GEORGE ORWELL

george
orwell

raymond williams

COLUMBIA UNIVERSITY PRESS/NEW YORK

Copyright © 1971 by Raymond Williams

Library of Congress Cataloging in Publication Data

Williams, Raymond.
  George Orwell.

  Reprint. Originally published: New York:
Viking Press, 1971. (Modern masters).
  Bibliography: p. 99
  Includes index.
  1. Orwell, George, 1903–1950—Criticism
and interpretation. I. Title.
[PR6029.R8Z86   1981]   828'.91209   81-6134
ISBN 0-231-05374-6   AACR2
ISBN 0-231-05375-4 (pbk.)
Library of Congress catalog card number: 71-132184

ACKNOWLEDGMENTS

  Brandt & Brandt: From: *Nineteen Eighty-four* by George Orwell.
Copyright, 1949, by Harcourt, Brace and World, Inc. Reprinted by
permission of Brandt & Brandt.

  Harcourt Brace Jovanovich, Inc.: Excerpts from George Orwell's
Homage to Catalonia and *The Road to Wigan Pier* and *Collected
Essays, Journalism and Letters of George Orwell* are reprinted by
permission of Harcourt Brace Jovanovich, Inc.; Copyright © 1968 by
Sonia Brownell Orwell.

  Reprinted by arrangement with the Viking Press.

  Columbia University Press Morningside Edition, 1981
  Columbia University Press
  New York

  Clothbound editions of Columbia University Press books are
Smyth-sewn and printed on permanent and durable acid-free paper.

  Printed in U.S.A.

p 10 9 8 7 6 5 4 3 2

CONTENTS

GEORGE ORWELL

i

Eric Arthur Blair was born in 1903, at Motihari, in British-occupied India. He was the second child of Richard Walmesley Blair and Ida Mabel Limouzin. His father, then aged 46, was an agent in the Opium Department of the Indian Civil Service. His paternal grandfather had served in the Indian Army and later became an Anglican clergyman. His maternal grandfather had been a teak merchant in Burma and later a rice-grower.

When Eric Blair was four the family returned to England and settled at Henley, though the father returned to India and served there until his retirement in 1912. Eric wrote later that he barely saw his father before he was eight. His mother, eighteen years younger than her husband, bore their third child in 1908. The family was then of two daughters and a son, born at five-year intervals.

At the age of eight, Eric Blair was sent to a private preparatory school in Sussex, and he lived there, except in the school holidays, until he was thirteen. He then went by scholarship to two private secondary schools: Wellington (for one term); Eton (for four-and-a-half years). He again lived in the schools except during holidays. When he left Eton, the family moved from Oxfordshire to Suffolk. Eric Blair joined the Indian Imperial Police and was trained in Burma. He served there for nearly five years and then in 1927, while home on leave, decided not to return. His resignation from the Imperial Police became effective on the first day of 1928.

Blair's life until he was twenty-four is in all its visible details a training for membership in the administrative middle class of imperialist Britain. His family, on both sides, had lived and worked in India and Burma, in the army, administration, and trade. His first adult work was directly within this pattern. He had, moreover, grown up with that absence of normal family life characteristic of an England that was primarily a home base and a network of ruling-class schools. When Blair broke the pattern in 1927, he found himself in an England where he had spent two-thirds of his life but always within institutions (or, more rarely, in a family situation) that defined a particular set of social relationships. The political and cultural dominance of men with similar backgrounds and histories has been so marked, in the first half of the twentieth century in Britain, that Blair's growing-up has been commonly described as normal and orthodox. In any other terms, including those of the lives of most people in Britain, it was in important ways strange and even alien. This needs to be remembered and emphasized as we look at the next nine years of his life. For what these amounted to was the making of a new set of social relationships and the creation, in an important sense, of a new social identity. This is the critical evolution of Blair into Orwell.

The reasons for the first break are undoubtedly complex, but two factors are evident. Blair had been clear, in his adolescence, that he wanted to become a writer. The Imperial Police was in this and other respects what he called an unsuitable profession. But there is also good evidence (though mainly from much later, when his mind had cleared) that he had come to understand and reject the imperialism he was serving. Imperialism, he wrote, at the end of his change, was an evil thing, and the sooner he chucked his job and got out of it the better.[1] Yet within its service his response was more complicated. He was stuck, as he later saw it, between hatred of the Empire he was serving and rage against the native people who opposed it and made his immediate job difficult. Theoretically, he says, he was all for the Burmese and all against their British oppressors. Practically he was at once opposed to the dirty work of imperialism and involved in it.

Some parts of this complex response continued through the rest of his life. Yet what is also crucial, at the time of the break, is his uncertain and ambiguous relationship to England: the country he knows and belongs to, yet in

[1] *Collected Essays, Journalism and Letters of George Orwell,* I, 236.
  Page references given in footnotes throughout this book, other than those citing the *Collected Essays*, are to the Uniform Edition of Orwell's writing published by Secker & Warburg, Ltd., London. American editions are listed in the bibliography at the end of this book.

other ways does not know at all except in abstraction. It would have been possible for him to leave the Imperial Police and settle in England within the class network of his heritage. If he had been reacting only against explicit imperialism, this might have been a normal course. But the problem of his position within England was more critical. What Blair actually did, in the first six months of his release, was to go on what he thought of as an expedition to the East End of London to get to know the English poor. He took as a base a room in Notting Hill. Then, in the spring of 1928, he took a room in a working-class district of Paris. His favorite aunt, Nellie Limouzin, had lived in the same road in Notting Hill and was living in Paris for the eighteen months of his stay there. The expedition to the East End was of a kind that he was later often to repeat: a journey of discovery of ordinary English people. But taking those first two-and-a-half years of his new life as a whole, it is reasonable to see as his main impulse his establishment as a writer. For that purpose the choice of Paris was characteristic of the time. Ten years later, he wrote that Paris in the late 1920s was "invaded by such a swarm of artists, writers, students, dilettanti, sight-seers, debauchees and plain idlers as the world has never seen . . . in some quarters of the town the so-called artists must actually have outnumbered the working population." Then "the slump descended like another Ice Age, the cosmopolitan mob of artists vanished."[2] We must notice the habit, characteristic of several phases of his experience, of writing in these contemptuous and devaluing terms of something of which he had himself been a part. He

[2] *Ibid.*, p. 493.

wrote two novels, which have been lost, during his time in Paris, and published some articles in French and English. He became ill with pneumonia, worked ten weeks as a dishwasher and kitchen porter, and then returned to England at the end of 1929.

For the next two-and-a-half years he worked to establish himself as a writer from a different base. He used his parents' home in Suffolk for writing and earned money from occasional articles and teaching. He completed several versions of what was to become his first book, called, not by his choice, *Down and Out in Paris and London.* "I would *rather* answer to 'dishwasher' than 'down and out.' "[3] The book was a record of his experiences, but "if it is all the same to everybody I would prefer [it] to be published pseudonymously." Since he was earning his living as a teacher when it was due to be published, one aspect of this preference is understandable. But the question of a name, and the deeper question of an identity, had arisen before. He was still going on what he thought of as expeditions in England: living with tramps, with hop-pickers, and in working-class districts. Discussing the publication of *Down and Out in Paris and London,* he wrote to his agent in late 1932:

> As to a pseudonym, a name I always use when tramping etc is P. S. Burton, but if you don't think this sounds a probable kind of name, what about
>
> > Kenneth Miles
> > George Orwell
> > H. Lewis Allways.

I rather favour George Orwell.[4]

[3] *Ibid.*, p. 107.
[4] *Ibid.*, p. 106.

The Orwell is a river in Suffolk, south of his parents' home.

This first book by Orwell was published in 1933. During the next three years he completed his establishment as a writer. He earned money from teaching, working in a bookshop, and reviewing, and began living for longer periods away from his parents' home. *Down and Out in Paris and London* was followed by the novel *Burmese Days*, published first in the United States rather than in England because of his English publisher's fear of its giving offense in Burma. Then came two more novels, *A Clergyman's Daughter*, published in 1935, and *Keep the Aspidistra Flying*, published in 1936. In the spring of 1936 he moved to a village store at Wallington, in Hertfordshire, and two months later married Eileen O'Shaughnessy, daughter of a customs collector, an Oxford graduate (1927) in English, a teacher and journalist, and later (1934) a London graduate student in psychology. They were Eric and Eileen Blair, but the recognizable identity of George Orwell had now, after the years of difficulty and transition, been clearly established.

Orwell's reputation at this time, as writer and journalist, was based mainly on his accounts of poverty and depression. His expeditions and then his convincing reports had given him a particular though limited identity in the literary world. He had first broken his orthodox social relationships and then, for irregular periods but consciously and recurrently, dropped out of them. What he brought back, into a class-conscious culture and at a time of general poverty and depression, were reports from a world that seemed as distant in experience as Burma. His next book was a commission in this precise identity: an inquiry, for the Left Book Club, into the life of the poor and unemployed.

But 1936, when he received this commission, was a year of crisis and change in a quite different dimension. While the commission prolonged his previous identity as a writer, his way of fulfilling it, in *The Road to Wigan Pier*, marked an entry to a new project, as a political writer, which was to last the rest of his life. For while the first part of the book is the kind of reporting that he had been asked for and that he could do so well, the second part is an essay on class and socialism that is effectively the first statement of Orwell's basic political position. Repeating his opposition to imperialism and the class system, he now adds a commitment to socialist definitions of freedom and equality while at the same time attacking most forms of the organized socialist movement and especially various kinds of English middle-class socialists.

He had made the journey to Lancashire and Yorkshire in February and March, before settling at Wallington and opening his shop in the afternoons. He was married in June, and during the summer and autumn wrote his book. But in July the Spanish Civil War broke out, and by the end of the autumn Orwell was preparing to go to Spain to collect material for articles and perhaps to fight. Soon after he had arrived in Barcelona he joined the militia of the POUM (Partido Obrero de Unificacion Marxista) and was in action with them in January 1937. He then transferred to the British Independent Labour Party contingent serving with the POUM militia, became a corporal and later a lieutenant, and was wounded in the middle of May. He had tried, in April, to join the In-

ternational Brigade in Madrid, but became involved in
the conflict between the Republican authorities and the
POUM, and again, after convalescence, was personally
involved in this when the POUM was declared illegal. He
got out into France in June.

This experience of war and revolutionary politics hardened his position in several ways. It did not make him an
anticommunist, since he had rejected Soviet-style communism as a possible commitment many years before.
Yet it was mainly his direct experience of communist-
POUM rivalry that sharpened his anticommunism to a
positive position. At the same time he became, and remained for the next two or three years, a revolutionary
socialist. *The Road to Wigan Pier* in which he had attacked most orthodox British socialist positions, including what he knew as Marxism, had been published in
March 1937 while he was at the front. As soon as he returned from Spain, he began writing *Homage to Catalonia*, which completed his break with the orthodox Left.
The book was published in April 1938, and in June Orwell
joined the Independent Labour Party, in which he stayed
until the early months of the war. He wanted to go to
India to write a new book, but he became ill with tuberculosis in the late winter of 1938 and was in a sanato-
rium until the late summer. With a loan from L. H.
Myers (author of *The Near and the Far*) he then went to
spend the winter in Morocco, returning to England in the
spring of 1939.

During the winter in Morocco he wrote his fourth
novel, *Coming Up for Air*. On his return to England he
wrote some of his best-known essays: on Dickens, on
Boys' Weeklies, and, as war was beginning, "Inside the

Whale." From Morocco he had been writing letters sketching the possibility of an underground antiwar Left as the only alternative to a slow drift into fascism in Britain. But when war began, he came to believe that "now we are in this bloody war we have got to win it and I would like to lend a hand."[5] He was rejected by the army as physically unfit, and was again short of money as opportunities for occasional journalism declined. He moved back to London in May 1940, and in the autumn of that year wrote "The Lion and the Unicorn," an essay subtitled "Socialism and the English Genius." From early 1941 he began writing "London Letters" for the American *Partisan Review*, and then in August joined the BBC as a talks producer in the Indian section of the Eastern Service, where he stayed until late 1943. He served for a time in the Home Guard and as a fire-watcher.

The year 1943 was in several ways a turning point. In March Orwell's mother died. He had to leave the Home Guard because he was ill, and he left the BBC to become literary editor of the *Tribune*, then directed by Aneurin Bevan. He took on more regular book-reviewing, but the decisive event was that late in the year he began writing *Animal Farm*. Completed by February 1944, it was rejected by several publishers on political grounds. It did not appear until August 1945, at the end of the war.

Toward the end of the war in Europe, Orwell traveled to France and later to Germany and Austria as a reporter. He and his wife had adopted a son in 1944, but in March 1945 his wife died during an operation. He kept the child, and later in the year made his first journey to the

[5] *Ibid.*, p. 410.

island of Jura, off the Scottish coast. In 1946 he settled there, with his younger sister as housekeeper, though returning to London for the winter. His elder sister had died in 1946, and his own health was getting steadily worse. During 1947, in the early months of renewed tuberculosis, he wrote the first draft of *Nineteen Eighty-four* and in 1948, amid several attacks, wrote the second draft. By the end of that year he was very seriously ill and was to write hardly anything else.

The extraordinary commercial success of *Animal Farm* ended the financial worries from which he had suffered, as a writer, since that time of decision nearly twenty years earlier when he left the Imperial Police. But by the time this happened he was already into his last years of recurrent illness and pain. In September 1949 he went into hospital in London, and in October married Sonia Brownell. In January 1950 he died.

England, Whose England?

11

"England, my England," wrote Lawrence. "England, your England," wrote Orwell.

Orwell wrote two long essays about England: "The Lion and the Unicorn" in 1940, and "The English People" in 1944. Near the beginning of each, he introduces the viewpoint of someone arriving in England. "When you come back to England from any foreign country, you have immediately the sensation of breathing a different air." "It is worth trying for a moment to put oneself in the position of a foreign observer, new to England, but unprejudiced, and able because of his work to keep in touch with ordinary, useful, unspectacular people."[1] This may seem no more than a literary device. Much of Orwell's writing about England is so close and detailed, his emphasis on ordinary English

[1] *Collected Essays, . . . ,* II, 57; III, 1.

virtues so persistent, that he is now often seen as the archetypal Englishman, the most native and English of writers. But it is necessary to remember the real history: the creation of Orwell from Blair. Many of the ways in which he sees England are affected and sometimes determined by his history: born, educated, and taking his first job in a ruling-class network that was in some deliberate ways cut off from ordinary England; rejecting this network and setting out on his own to discover the country for himself. Similarly, many of the ways in which he values English life are affected and determined by this journey. His notable attachment to what he saw as ordinary England is an act not so much of membership as of conscious affiliation.

We shall see how this affected his deepest imagination and his values. But we need to look first at the England to which he was reacting in this special way. For there was one noteworthy advantage in his history: that he came to look at England with a knowledge of its Empire, a point of view on this insular society which was in many ways penetrating.

"Not Counting Niggers" he wrote in 1939, about a plan for a European Federal Union geographically similar (and thence politically similar) to what we now know as NATO and the Common Market. In a convenient oversight, the existence of a huge colonial population controlled by this bloc had been left out of the plan. "What we always forget is that the overwhelming bulk of the British proletariat does not live in Britain but in Asia and Africa. . . . This is the system which we all live on."[2] And as he writes elsewhere: "I was in the

[2] *Ibid.*, I, 397.

Indian Police five years, and by the end of that time I hated the imperialism I was serving with a bitterness which I probably cannot make clear. In the free air of England that kind of thing is not fully intelligible. In order to hate imperialism you have got to be part of it."[3]

The eyes of the observer, of the man coming back to England, are eyes full of this experience of imperialism. But he is not coming to England in the same way as, say, an Indian or an African student: to a foreign country about which he has only read. He has been educated here; his family lives here. He is aware of the internal structure of English society, but from a class position that he has only theoretically rejected. At school, he said, he had had "no notion that the working class were human beings. At a distance . . . I could agonise over their sufferings, but I still hated them and despised them when I came anywhere near them. . . . To the shock-absorbers of the bourgeoisie, such as myself, 'common people' still appeared brutal and repulsive."[4]

This very special position, a kind of conscious double vision, is central to Orwell. It has been overlooked, time and again, by people reading back from his later reporting, and especially by people who shared his kind of childhood and education but who did not undergo his subsequent direct revulsion from imperialism. It is impossible to convince most people who had Orwell's kind of separated education that they are not, in the most central ways, English. For of course the definition of "England," its myth and its ideology, has been for more than a century in just their hands. This is the class that does most

[3] *The Road to Wigan Pier*, p. 145.
[4] *Ibid.*, pp. 142–43.

of the writing, that directs not only its own but most other institutions, and that, traveling abroad, is known to most of the world as "the English." A world-view of England, we can fairly say, has been based on the character of this tiny minority.

Yet it is not, as a minority, without its internal differences. It is necessary to describe it as a ruling class, and at that time the ruling class of an Empire. But only part of the class was quite wholly in command: able to live on its property and investments, or to move directly into the central metropolitan institutions. A much larger part had a harder and humbler function. The education of these people, essentially, was as servants of a system to which they belonged only as functionaries. And it was they who went out to the edges of the system, facing its realities directly. Eric Blair was born into what he later called, in exactly this sense, the "lower upper-middle-class." Theoretically a member of the ruling class and sharing its insistent myth and ideology of "England," he and men like him were in practice on the outer edge of the system. Owning no land or substantial property, they were dependent on their professional salaries, which were in turn dependent on accepting the definitions of "profession" and "service" that the system as a whole had created. Often, in such a group, there is a kind of overadjustment to the very myths that offer to define membership in the class as a whole. The fear of dropping out of the class of which such men are literally the bottom edge can produce more rigid and more blatant definitions of their "England" than might be found at the relaxed and comfortable center. Eric Blair's first appearance in print, at the age of eleven, was with a characteristic poem: "Awake! Young Men of England." He was a boy miming a role.

Seen from outside, as most of us must now see it, this position generates a particular tension: that of the man who is simultaneously dominator and dominated. The tension can be overlaid by a miming rigidity that can come to serve as the whole personality. Or it can lead, as in Blair's case, to crisis: the crisis which made him into Orwell. And then the double vision, rooted in the simultaneous positions of dominator and dominated, is at once powerful and disturbed.

When he re-entered England, that is to say, his primary impulse was negative: a rejection of the system and the ideology in which he had been educated and in which he served. But because of the character of the system, there was no other "England" to which he could immediately go. He could only drop out of one England and make expeditions to the other. When he summed all this up toward the end of his journey, what he had to say was affected as much by the character of the negation as by the character of the subsequent and conscious affiliation:

I felt that I had got to escape not merely from imperialism but from every form of man's dominion over man. I wanted to submerge myself, to get right down among the oppressed, to be one of them and on their side against their tyrants. . . . It was in this way that my thoughts turned towards the English working class. It was the first time that I had ever been really aware of the working class, and to begin with it was only because they supplied an analogy.

They were the symbolic victims of injustice, playing the same part in England as the Burmese played in Burma.[5]

This, very clearly, and described with his usual frankness, is that form of *negative identification* in which approach and affiliation to a new group is a function of the subject's initial and formative social experience.

England, whose England? In *The Road to Wigan Pier* the sense of the journey is still active: Orwell is describing the "two nations," discovering how (in that middle-class phrase) the other half lives. He is at once compassionate and indignant, drawn and repelled. He is describing a country in which two-thirds of the population are working-class people at a time of depression and wide-spread unemployment. All his active arguments and images are of contrasts, intolerable contrasts. "England," as any simple idea, has been destroyed by these contrasts. The single image of his childhood has been replaced by the particularities, the variations, the inequalities of mine and mill, slum and councilhouse, caravan site and slag-heap, teashop and Tudor villa. This is an active England, an England to move through.

The England of the later essays, written in wartime, is different. It is not necessarily more true or false, but it is again, in some significant ways, single: "Economically, England is certainly two nations, if not three or four. But at the same time the vast majority of the people *feel* themselves to be a single nation and are conscious of resembling one another more than they resemble foreigners."[6] That, perhaps, is not very surprising. It would pre-

5 *Ibid.*, pp. 149–50.
6 *Collected Essays,* . . . , II, 64.

sumably be true of any long-settled country. But in and through this unexceptionable observation, something else is being said.

> England is the most class-ridden country under the sun. It is a land of snobbery and privilege, ruled largely by the old and silly. But in any calculation about it one has got to take into account its emotional unity, the tendency of nearly all its inhabitants to feel alike and act together in moments of supreme crisis.[7]

The final clause of the passage, written in 1940 at a time of exceptional national unity under the threat of invasion, is more obviously acceptable than the preceding description of "emotional unity," which makes a much larger claim. "England is . . . but . . ." is the recurring pattern of this argument, leading to a particular climax which comes "as near as one can . . . to describing England in a phrase: a family with the wrong members in control."

Now Orwell was neither the first nor the last to say something like this. The statement's interest is in where it comes on the scale of his development. There is not much sense of a family or emotional unity in the depressed and suffering England of *The Road to Wigan Pier*. The emphasis there is on the realities and consequences of a class society. What happens, I think, is that Orwell first moves through two phases of response to "England": the myth of his boyhood, the special people, the "family," is succeeded by the observations made on his return—a scene of bitter and bleak contradictions. But then, in a third phase, he creates a new myth that until quite recently has remained effective. Qualifying

[7] *Ibid.*, p. 67.

the original image with the facts of economic and social inequality, he creates the sense of an England of basic ordinariness and decency, a "real England," "an ever-lasting animal stretching into the future and the past," in which it can be seen almost as an accident, or at least as an evident archaism, that the "wrong members" of the family are in control.

Orwell's great influence since the 1940s owes as much to this powerful image as to any other single achievement. And it would not be so powerful if it did not contain some truth. Orwell's emphasis on the depth of civil liberties in Britain and on the feelings that support them is, in the world as he knew it and as we continue to know it, justified. His further emphasis on the gentleness and mildness of much ordinary English life, on these qualities being positive achievements in a world of killing and anger, is again reasonable. Certain kinds of informality, friendliness, and tolerance in much of everyday English life support his emphasis on "decency" as a virtue. But it is possible to know and acknowledge all these things and still, in analysis, go either way.

Orwell is nearest to what I believe to be the truth when he describes these characteristics as parts of a genuinely popular culture that "must live to some extent *against* the existing order."[8] Or again, when he speaks of a "subtle network of compromises" and adjustments through which certain virtues, certain achievements, are maintained alongside certain evident and radical injustices. But as we begin to define in these ways, we find that we are discussing very complicated relationships within a very complicated social structure. Orwell recog-

[8] *Ibid.*, p. 59.

nizes and emphasizes the complexity, but he does not develop any kind of thinking that can sustain and extend a critical analysis of structures. The evidence is collected, often in sharp detail, and the sense of a climate, an atmosphere, is memorably created. But a social structure is not a climate. It can never be enough to say that certain virtues exist *alongside* certain injustices, as if they were contrasting facts of the natural world (on which, in his social imagery, Orwell so commonly draws). In a society, these facts are relationships of an active, historical, and developing kind. And it is this kind of reality that Orwell's image of "England" obscures.

That is a fact about his method. But, as so often, the method ultimately depends on a point of view. Orwell's way of describing the faults of this "family" with the "wrong members" in control has again been influential. Class, for example, is described mainly in terms of differences and snobberies in accent, clothes, tastes, furnishing, food. And this has become habitual. In *The Road to Wigan Pier* the sinking middle class, realizing the identity of their interests with the exploited working class, would have "nothing to lose but our aitches." Correspondingly, in the milder world of "The Lion and the Unicorn," the prosperous workers are becoming "visibly . . . more middle-class." In this way of thinking Orwell prepared the orthodox political climate of a generation. For of course it is true that if class means only these differences in private social behavior, differences that are often little more than external and trivial, a certain "classlessness" is inevitable in conditions of growing prosperity and extended education and communications. The difference from the old overt and vulgar display of class distinction is something any reasonable person would welcome. But by keeping the definition of class to these characteristics, which any prosperous industrial society will in any case erode, another set of facts, in which class is a powerful and continuing economic relationship—as between the owners of property and capital and the owners only of labor and skill—is effectively masked.

For what is it, after all, that puts the "wrong members of the family" in control? Is it only a deference to their accents, their clothes, their styles of eating and furnishing? It is strange to have to make this point about an Orwell whose emphasis on the determining fact of money is so intense and even at times (in the 1930s) extreme. But there's money in the pocket, and more money in more pockets will mean precisely the classlessness he refers to. There's also, however, that quite different "money" that is capital, that is the ownership and creation of the means of social life itself. Here the question about control is inevitably a question about this ownership, which can indeed remain unaltered in any major way during a period in which the visible signs of "class," the small change of the system, have been if not wiped out (for there is no sign of that happening, thirty years after Orwell wrote) at least modified, moderated, and evolved.

The clearest sign of the weakness of Orwell's description—but also, as it happens, of its appeal—can be seen in his discussion of what he still calls the ruling class. Here his initial attitudes are complicated, for the reasons discussed earlier. He sees his own group, the service families, pushed down in importance by the growth of centralized bureaucracy and by the monopoly trading companies. Their vitality and initiative, he thinks, have declined since the high point of Empire in the years just before he was born. At the same time, a part of the same class has become not merely frustrated but disaffected. This is his regular description of English middle-class intellectuals, especially Left intellectuals: shallow, negative, and out of touch with and against their own country.

But these he sees as the outriders. in the ruling-class family but now either as its servants or as its black sheep. The core of the ruling class is still there, and what is most remarkable about it, he says, is its stupidity. In terms of the family, that is, England, these are the "irresponsible uncles and bedridden aunts"; the image, as it happens, admits no father.

It is a beguiling picture. What happened in the ruling class, according to Orwell, was a decay of ability. Its position "had long ceased to be justifiable." An "aristocracy constantly recruited from parvenus . . . there they sat, at the centre of a vast empire and a world-wide financial network, drawing interest and profits and spending them— on what?" On nothing useful, to be sure. "Only half a million people, the people in the country houses, definitely benefitted from the existing system."[9] True enough, but what is remarkable is that this is seen as the "decay" of a ruling class, as if that gang of aristocrats recruited from parvenus had *ever* had any different or more justifiable social aims. And the only real test of their "ability" would be, surely, their capacity to continue to impose themselves.

It is much easier to despise the ruling class than to

[9] *Ibid.*, pp. 69–70.

hate and break it. Orwell's comic uncles and aunts are a recurring radical image, but to see the actual ruling class in that way is in the end an indulgence, dependent emotionally on that very middle-class image of England as a family. Once again, the naïve myth has been qualified by some of its unacknowledged consequences and then, in a more acceptable form, in part restored. "Long ceased to be justifiable"—that presupposes an original justification, when the aristocracy was not bumbling and stupid but able, daring, and ruthless. It is a radical illusion and a radical rhetoric that in its sentimental and indulgent underestimate has always weakened the British Left. Orwell was nearer to the facts of the society he was observing, and nearer to the necessary response to them, when he wrote, with an anger he usually reserved for his enemies on the Left, of "the rat-trap faces of bankers and the brassy laughter of stockbrokers," against which all social criticism broke.

The difficulty, then, lies in the original image of a family. Orwell hated what he saw of the consequences of capitalism, but he was never able to see it, fully, as an economic and political *system*. His great strength in personalizing particular injustices was not supported by any adequate understanding of the very general forces involved. He wanted, deeply and genuinely, to bring "the real England" to the surface, to turn the war into "a revolutionary war," both defeating fascism and finishing capitalism. In part this program is the understandable rhetoric of 1940, and it was quite widely shared throughout the war years. But inside it there is a whole view of the system being opposed—an influential view, right through to the Labour governments of the 1960s—that has now shown its inadequacy. The old system, with its aristocratic and parvenu stupidities, is seen as a top layer that must be replaced with "new blood, new men, new ideas." The spread of the middle class is seen as having made the old class analysis almost obsolete, and the working class anyway is believed to be rapidly acquiring middle-class habits and ideas. The ruling class are seen as having become mere owners, their work done for them by managers and technicians. All that is then needed, it seems, is for all the decent members of the family—middle class and working class alike—to get rid of the outdated old fools in charge.

Trumpets around the walls of the barbican. Trumpets turning into penny-whistles and then, reflected in the new shining glass, suddenly and surprisingly accompanied by a respectful and celebratory choir.

It is not Orwell's fault that he did not foresee the "England, England" of advanced capitalism. But it is a fact that he popularized a version of England—all the more effective because it was a version and not a theory, a mood rather than an analysis susceptible of disproof—that in some of its very strengths and pertinence has been in practice disarming.

"A foreign observer, new to England." He was never, of course, that. But he came back from the periphery with a real and lasting hatred of imperialism and saw at the center what his education and experience had prepared him for: "a family with the wrong members in control." The fact is, he needed this family. He had been deprived of it, humiliated by it. Now he acted out the humiliation, trying to speak to and rally the other members of the family, trying to get them to take over.

What he could tell them about effectively was the imperialism they ignored, the slums they neglected. But just as it is limiting to see a capitalist system without its imperialist extension, so it is limiting to see capitalism only through imperialism and through its visible ruling class. Part of the England Orwell discovered was a real society, living under and within this order, keeping certain values going. But inseparable from this was the different England created by this order, in prejudices, compromises, adjustment, illusions. To respond to the society would be to distinguish one part from the other, to enter a necessary conflict reaching into every area of life. But to do that to a family, to "England," would be unthinkable: treacherous and mean. He has lost a family and its old family pride. He is trying to join a family, to take part in a decent future. The emotions are understandable and honorable, but they are particular emotions—the emotions of the exile from a lost country, a lost class. Seen from where "England" is happening, stretching to past and future in its more immediate and complicated processes, they are too easy, too settling, too sweet.

For "England, my England" is an assertion, a declaration of independence, a challenge. "England, your England," by contrast, is a version, a story, a dream. And when it breaks, under pressure, it will become a nightmare.

Being a Writer

What did it mean, in Orwell's generation, to be a writer? The question can seem naïve. Many people think that being a writer carries its own simple and self-evident definition. Yet any such definition turns out, on analysis, to have a social history; it is an idea like any other.

In Orwell's case the definition is particularly important, not only as a way of understanding his achievement and his influence, but also as a way of seeing a particular kind of literary crisis, itself clearly part of a social crisis occurring at just the historical moment when he was learning to write.

It was the late 1920s. Seven years later Orwell wrote:

On the last occasion when *Punch* produced a genuinely funny joke, which was only six or

> seven years ago, it was a picture of an intolerable youth telling his aunt that when he came down from the University he intended to 'write'. 'And what are you going to write about, dear?', his aunt enquires. 'My dear aunt,' the youth replies crushingly, 'one doesn't write *about* anything, one just *writes*'.[1]

Orwell goes on to say that the cartoon was a "perfectly justified criticism of current literary cant." But this is in 1936. In fact the problem was one that he was never quite sure about, and that the state of literary argument in his period didn't help him to resolve. He was always likely, for example, even late in his life, to make a distinction of *intention* between the writing of prose and the writing of verse. This turns out, on examination, to be a distinction between writing for the effect of the content and writing for the effect of the words. In prose, though not in all prose, the former is assumed to predominate.

But this distinction itself is the product of a divided aesthetics. Language, characteristically, is taken to be an agent rather than a source of experience. Or, to put it another way, content is taken to precede language, and the writer can then choose whether to reveal content directly or to work with words for their own sake. Even if this is only a matter of emphasis rather than a rigid distinction, it is profoundly misleading. For it is always the *relation* between experience and expression, in an individual writer and in the language and forms that he shares with his society, that is really decisive.

Orwell kept coming back to this problem as he tried to direct and understand his development. In "Why I Write" (1946) he described his early development, from fantasies

[1] *Collected Essays, . . . ,* I, 256–57.

with himself as hero to what he calls "more and more a mere description of what I was doing and the things I saw." That "mere" is significant. For it is repeated in what he sees as the next stage in his adolescent development, when he suddenly discovered "the joy of mere words, i.e., the sounds and associations of words." Mere description, mere words. This way of seeing the literary problem remained important not only in his development, but as one characteristic form of the underlying social crisis of his time.

What is most significant is the desire to justify himself as a writer: that problem of justification, and of seriousness, that the remembered joke had stirred into activity. He was living, after all, at a time and within a class in which the whole practice of writing was problematic. Leaving aside "writing for entertainment"—the production of a written commodity that others would consume and, if it was pleasing, value—attitudes to writing had hardened and even polarized. In the confident middle class, intent on its version of practicality, writing was thought of as an impractical secondary activity, an alternative to "doing something real." Characteristically, of course, an escape route was allowed at that point where the impractical activity had practical effects; that is to say, made money. The successful author (a rather different character from the simple "writer") was then an admired and rewarded producer, like any other. But there was not only the difficulty of stages, of getting from being a writer to being a successful author. There was also the fact that on this projection the writer had no autonomous purposes: his definition of achievement would be shaped from the beginning by an external and alienated standard. At the same time, a growing minority of the same social class made a related but apparently opposite abstraction in reaction to this. If the only orthodox test of achievement was "social" recognition and success, then this could be "opposed" by a simple negation. The "writer," the true writer, had no commercial aims, but also, at root, no social function and, by derivation, no social content. He just "wrote." And then as a self-defined recognizable figure, he lived "outside" society—unconventional, the "artist."

This development and polarization had a real social history. It was an important phase of nineteenth-century bourgeois life and thought, reaching its first climax in the 1880s and 1890s in most of Europe, and was still active though hardened and at times conventional in the 1920s. It has many effects, in theory and in practice. It is at the root of the conventional distinction between "content" and "form" in their effective modern senses. Orwell's theoretical questions, never pushed far enough to become genuine theory, are also practical reactions to the immediate crisis of what he was to do. There are several reasons for his conscious rejection of the conventional life of his class: an attempted social identification with its victims; a search for an identity beyond its determined figures; a refusal of what it understood as success. But there is also, at least at first, a simpler reaction, taking up one of the prepared alternative roles. It is in this sense, I would say, that he goes to Paris to "be a writer"; that is to say, to live "outside" society and to "write." Recalling that period, in "Inside the Whale" he repeats his memory of the *Punch* joke; recalls the "swarm of artists, writers, students, dilettanti, sight-seers, debauchees and plain idlers"; and describes its ideology: "In cultured circles art-for-art's-saking extended practically to a worship of the meaningless. Literature was supposed to consist solely in the manipulation of words."[2] Perhaps this is overstated. It is a late generalization. But it is an interesting way of seeing the form of the literary and social crisis through which he developed.

Orwell's choice as a writer, we may now see, was in quite the other direction from that emphasis of the 1920s. It can be said that he chose content before form, experience before words; that he became the socially conscious writer of the 1930s rather than the aesthetic writer of the 1920s. Certainly, to an important extent, that is how he saw it himself. But then, just as important, seeing the choice in this way, he sometimes regretted it. In "Why I Write," for example, he said that a writer has four motives: sheer egoism, aesthetic enthusiasm, historical impulse, political purpose. These sometimes contradict each other, and in degree and proportion will vary in all writers and in any writer according to his period. In a different age, he said, the first three motives would, for him, have outweighed the fourth. He would have written "ornate or merely descriptive books." But "as it is I have been forced into becoming a sort of pamphleteer."[3] What is interesting there is "forced." He has a clear idea of himself as he might have been in a different time. He could then see his actual writing as in some ways a contradiction of his nature: "taking your 'nature' to be the state you have attained when you are first

2 *Ibid.*, p. 508.
3 *Ibid.*, p. 4.

adult."[4] This is not a hypothetical nature in some quite different time. It is a "nature" with a precise period reference, to when he was first adult, in the twenties.

What has then happened, if we accept this account, is a virtual invasion of his natural self, his natural writing, by an inevitable social and political reality. That he sees it as inevitable is of course important. How could a man, a writer, stand aside when such things were happening? But the form of this acknowledgment remains interesting. For it presupposes a situation in which a writer could choose whether to be exposed to a social and political reality; the bitterness of the 1930s was that no decent man could choose not to be exposed.

But this is only a repetition in a particular form of his original and, I would say, persistent world-view. Men have their natures—not innate natures but their formed adult selves—which a social and political reality invades. Orwell's apparently limited statement about writing turns out, on reflection, to be a very general statement about individuals and societies. The relation between "writing" and "reality" is a form of the relation between men and their history.

Eric Blair, indeed, might have become somebody else: not Orwell but X. The choice of Orwell—not the name but the actual work—was made within a very pressing general and personal history. He developed as a writer through the years of the Depression and of fascism. At every point in these years he exposed himself to these facts in their most direct form. He became unemployed and penniless, partly because of the early difficulties of

[4] *Ibid.*

being a writer but also deliberately, as a way of cutting his connections with an established and unacceptable social position. He went to Spain to fight fascism, partly, to begin with, as a way of being a writer but then deliberately, as a way of setting his life against an evil and destructive social force. His courage and persistence in this repeated exposure to the hardest facts of his time are by any standard remarkable. Yet in and through this exposure there is an unresolved problem: that of the other self, the other writer, that he had wished and still wished to be.

The force of the desire was the whole problem. Many men, many writers, have been "invaded"; broken in on by a history that they did not choose and that, though disturbing and troubling, remained external to them. This is not, obviously, Orwell's case. The "invasion" was actively sought, indeed invited. And yet behind it, all the time—behind this inevitable "content"—was another image, other words; another way of "being a writer." Orwell eventually generalized this problem in the late essay "Writers and Leviathan":

> The invasion of literature by politics was bound to happen. It must have happened, even if the special problem of totalitarianism had never arisen, because we have developed a sort of compunction which our grandparents did not have, an awareness of the enormous injustice and misery of the world, and a guilt-stricken feeling that one ought to be doing something about it, which makes a purely aesthetic attitude towards life impossible. No one, now, could devote himself to literature as single-mindedly as Joyce or Henry James.[5]

[5] *Ibid.*, IV, 408–409.

This account of the invasion is significant. Totalitarianism, active interference with writers, is a special problem, but underlying it is something more general, a social conscience. And that is an invasion? Orwell usually describes his own feelings so accurately that surface analysis is hardly ever necessary; he seems to say very clearly what he means. But here he is saying that the "social conscience" of the writer, hitherto detached but now necessarily involved, is an invasion of "literature." And, characteristically, his definition of literature, if only as something now unattainable, is still related to "a purely aesthetic attitude towards life." His example of Joyce doesn't help. Joyce wrote as he did through poverty and exile. *Finnegans Wake* was completed in 1939. That emphasis, right or wrong, was historically available. But the example of James is extremely suggestive, for it takes us back to the period when not this problem but this way of stating the problem became normal.

Reading Orwell's account quickly, one might never remember the English novelists from Dickens and Elizabeth Gaskell to George Eliot and Hardy: those contemporaries of "our grandparents" who were indeed aware of "the enormous injustice and misery of the world" and who in different ways made literature from just this experience. There is nothing especially new about social awareness in writers, and indeed in the nineteenth century it-had been widespread and growing, especially among the novelists. But near the end of the century, and in England in relation to Henry James, an opposition between the "social" and the "aesthetic" was widely attempted. Not only was social experience seen as content and literature as form; also, and more dangerously, social experience was seen as only general and abstract, with the result that the definition of literary content was itself narrowed to an emphasis on abstracted "personal relationships." This, by the way, has little to do with James's actual work, in which social and personal experiences, though certainly in a limited world, were seen as interacting and at times integral. But in his emphasis on "handling" material, on the application of "manner" to "matter," James extended an understandable consciousness of technique to a point at which the wholly abstracted "aesthetic" emphasis could seem to be reasonably made. The important quarrel between James and Wells— between a composed, pure, essentially passive art, and new kinds of projected, committed, essentially purposive writing—came at a time when the development of the novel in twentieth-century conditions was very much at issue. A deeper awareness of psychological complexities was present, at the same time as a deeper awareness of social complexities. What was common was a sense of crisis, but alternative ways of describing it were in practice, each in its own fashion, each leading to radical changes in literary form yet pulling in quite opposite directions.

There was, then, a real and major problem in aesthetics, in which decisions about form were inseparable from decisions about experience. But this central issue, which is still not resolved, was overlaid by a kind of capture of terms, in which "aesthetic" and even "literature" were associated with only one of the possible decisions. Other possible and actual decisions were described, externally, as "anti-aesthetic" or "sociological." As this serious argument moved into the cant of the hangers-on, a situation was created in which even an Orwell could talk of an "aesthetic attitude towards life" that self-evidently excluded social conscience or even social consciousness. The aesthetic attitude that mattered was of course toward art: toward its substantial, serious, and varying problems. The "aesthetic attitude towards life" was a displaced consciousness relating to one of many possible artistic decisions but above all related to a version of society: not an artistic consciousness but a disguised social consciousness in which the real connections and involvements with others could be plausibly overlooked and then in effect ratified: a definition of "being a writer" that excluded social experience and social concern.

Orwell tried hard and seriously to reject the thinking of the social class in which he was educated. In a number of ways and at great personal cost he succeeded. But, ironically, the man who in practice solved some of these literary problems in an effective and often influential way continued to think not only that he was not solving them (a feeling natural enough to any continuing writer) but that in some way he was evading or abandoning literature: "a sort of pamphleteering," as he said with the sneer he had been taught.

His decisions needed to be integral, for at root they were one decision. The "aesthetic attitude towards life" was not only a way of writing novels of a particular kind. It was also, in effect, a formula, even a kind of treaty coming at just that point in the bourgeois reduction of art that was so critical in the twentieth-century experience. We can see, looking back, how convenient it was (how convenient if often still is) to put literature into a compartment in which, to be true to itself, it should have no direct concern with social reality. This suited the people who despised literature as impractical but who in any case wanted no independent scrutiny of any kind of the society they were actively directing and creating. Behind the simple words of the philistine there are quite often the harder words of the controller or censor. But then the apparent opposition—the people who said they valued literature—had in practice reduced it to a safe area and, moreover, were teaching attitudes that would limit its uses to touching and tasting. No real art of whatever kind could be reduced in this way, but what mattered, in the general consciousness, was not works but attitudes—a set of emphases, omissions, encouragements, discouragements, advice, warnings. How effective this set was we can see from Orwell's regretting the development that was in fact his achievement, hating the orthodox literary world but still carrying its instructions around in his mind to nag at and weaken his creative energy.

There is another problem: Orwell's complicated responses to the modern literature he valued and his uses of some of its methods in his own work. We shall look at this in some detail in the next chapter as we trace his literary development. But something more needs to be said here about the "invasion" of political and social reality, the forcibly altered definition of "being a writer." I have said that his decisions needed to be integral; that his social and political decisions—his refusal to live as an imperialist official or as the home-based equivalent—were profoundly connected with his decisions about writing. There was the failure I have noted: to rid himself of the assumptions about literature that he was in practice contradicting. But there was also something else, which lies very deep in his work and which may be the fundamental reason for what was otherwise only a superficial failure.

It would be easy to say that almost all Orwell's important writing is about someone who gets away from an oppressive normality. From the central characters of *The Clergyman's Daughter* and *Keep the Aspidistra Flying* to those of *Coming Up for Air* and *Nineteen Eighty-four*, this experience of awareness, rejection, and flight is repeatedly enacted. Yet it would be truer to say that most of Orwell's important writing is about someone who tries to get away but fails. That failure, that reabsorption, happens, in the end, in all the novels mentioned, though of course the experience of awareness, rejection, and flight has made its important mark.

The real paradox of Orwell may, then, be more clearly seen. Without the act of awareness and rejection he would not, probably, have been a writer at all. Most of his emphasis, understandably, is on that. But what if he felt, all the time, that in just this movement he was destined to fail? What if he felt, simultaneously, that the flight was necessary but also useless?

This would explain a good deal. For Orwell is then not only the man and the writer setting out on a new path but also, could it not be, the man and the writer whose "nature" has been invaded by an unwelcome reality, who has to live and write in these ways but who would have preferred other ways? An image of what he might have been under some other name (the renaming is crucial) is there and persists, while what he is and has chosen to be is very different. And the stress falls, necessarily, on "chosen." What Orwell consciously made of himself under very real pressures can be seen as an invasion of his nature not only because of the difficulty of the choice and its break from what he had been intended to be, but also because he felt, against much of the evidence, that he would in any case fail, that he would be dragged back, reabsorbed, into the powerful orthodox world. "Being a writer," in one definition, had been a possible way out. But being the writer he was, the real writer, led him into every kind of difficulty, every tension that the choice had seemed to offer to avoid.

Observation and Imagination

IV

Orwell's writing in the 1930s can be conventionally divided between the "documentary" and "factual" work on one hand, and the "fictional" and "imaginative" work on the other. The surface distinction is evident enough: on one hand *Down and Out in Paris and London, The Road to Wigan Pier, Homage to Catalonia,* and such sketches as "The Spike," "A Hanging," "Shooting an Elephant"; on the other hand the four novels *Burmese Days, A Clergyman's Daughter, Keep the Aspidistra Flying,* and *Coming Up for Air.* Yet nothing is clearer, as we look into the work as a whole, than that this conventional division is secondary. The key problem, in all this work, is the relation between "fact" and "fiction": an uncertain relation that is part of the whole crisis of "being a writer."

Literature used not to be divided in these

external ways. The rigid distinction between "documentary" and "imaginative" writing is a product of the nineteenth century, and most widely distributed in our own time. Its basis is a naïve definition of the "real world," and then a naïve separation of it from the observation and imagination of men. If there is real life and its recording, on one hand, and a separable imaginative world on the other, two kinds of literature can be confidently distinguished, and this is much more than a formal effect. In naturalist and positivist theories, this effective dualism of "the world" and "the mind" is at least clearly recognizable. But the conventional dualism of most orthodox literary theory has scarcely been noted, let alone challenged. Terms like "fiction" and "nonfiction," "documentary" and "imaginative," continue to obscure many of the actual problems of writing.

The unity of Orwell's "documentary" and "imaginative" writing is the very first thing to notice. There were many problems of method, but at least Orwell got past the conventional division, if only in practice. And he saw the division as it actually presented itself to him as something more than a formal problem. He correctly saw it as a problem of social relationships.

> English fiction on its higher levels is for the most part writen by literary gents about literary gents for literary gents; on its lower levels it is generally the most putrid "escape" stuff—old maids' fantasies about Ian Hay male virgins, or little fat men's visions of themselves as Chicago gangsters. Books about ordinary people behaving in an ordinary manner are extremely rare, because they can only be written by someone who is capable of standing both inside and outside the ordinary man, as Joyce for instance stands

inside and outside Bloom; but this involves admitting that you yourself *are* an ordinary person for nine-tenths of the time, which is exactly what no intellectual ever wants to do.[1]

There is still some unnoticed class feeling in this. Orwell is still seeing from far enough outside to suppose that there are people—a class of people—who are "ordinary" ten-tenths of the time. But to have got as far as he did is something.

> I think the interest of Bloom is that he is an ordinary uncultivated man described from within by someone who can also stand outside him and see him from another angle. Not that Bloom is an absolutely typical man in the street. . . .
> The man in the street is usually described in fiction either by writers who are themselves intellectually men in the street, tho' they may have great gifts as novelists (e.g. Trollope), or by cultivated men who describe him *from outside* (e.g. Samuel Butler, Aldous Huxley).[2]

Cultivated men who describe the man in the street from outside. It is in and through this social deformity, inflicted on him by his class and education, that Orwell reaches for the idea of an extended or even common humanity. His writing in the 1930s is an exploration, in experience and in books, toward such a humanity.

The problem of social relationship is, then, a problem of form. *Down and Out in Paris and London* is in effect a journal. What is put in is the experience of being without money in a modern city: the experience of dishwashers and tramps, of filthy rooms, dosshouses, casual

---

[1] *Collected Essays*, . . . , I, 230.
[2] *Ibid.*, pp. 126, 128.

wards. The author is present, but only insofar as these things are happening to him along with others. His own character and motivations are sketched as briefly as those of anyone else met in the kitchen or on the road. He is neither "inside" nor "outside"; he is simply drifting *with* others—exceptionally close to them but within the fact that they are drifting, that this is *happening* to their bodies and minds.

But then compare *A Clergyman's Daughter*. It is a novel about a repressed girl who has a breakdown, goes vagrant, and eventually returns, via teaching, to where she started. Anyone who reads Orwell's other writing of the time will find most of the experiences of the novel elsewhere in other forms. The "Church Times" and the glue-and-brown-paper theatrical armor, and even the "moribund hag who stinks of mothballs and gin, and has to be more or less carried to and from the altar" are to be found in Chapter One of the novel and in Orwell's letters about himself.[3] Again, the girl going vagrant, the hop-picking, Ginger and Deafie, sleeping rough in Trafalgar Square: they are to be found in Chapter Two and the beginning of Chapter Three, and also in Orwell's diary, "Hop-Picking."[4] The point is not the external relation between the writer's "material" and his "process of creation." The interest is almost entirely in the method of handling the author's own presence: the intermediary character of the girl—"inside" when she is caught in the routines of church and teaching; "outside," even amnesiac, when she is drifting on the road. The attempted characterization of the girl as more than a surrogate

[3] *Ibid.*, pp. 103, 105, 101–102.
[4] *Ibid.*, pp. 52–71.

presence is at times serious and detailed, at times merely functional. But a *sustained* identity, through diversity and dislocation of experiences, cannot yet be realized. And it is interesting that at one point—the night scene in Trafalgar Square, in the first section of Chapter Three— Orwell makes a conscious literary experiment of a different, impersonal kind, which is very evidently derived from the night-town chapter in *Ulysses*—the novel that had been so much in his mind as an example. He remained pleased with this experiment, though coming to reject his book as a whole.

Orwell's affinity to Joyce—or attempted affinity—is not in our usual reading. The modern writers Orwell mentions most often, in his earlier period, are Wells, Bennett, Conrad, Hardy, Kipling. In 1940 he makes a different list—Joyce, Eliot, and Lawrence. This change of emphasis through the 1930s is quite normal and representative. Among earlier writers on his 1940 list, he names Shakespeare, Swift, Fielding, Dickens, Reade, Butler, Zola, and Flaubert. The critical interest in Shakespeare, Swift, and Dickens can be seen from his essays. But in the development of his own writing there are two opposite emphases: the detailed interest in *Ulysses* (notably in a letter to Brenda Salkeld) at just the time of working on *A Clergyman's Daughter*, and also, as he said in 1940, "I believe the modern writer who has influenced me most is Somerset Maugham, whom I admire immensely for his power of telling a story straightforwardly and without frills."[5]

The names as such do not greatly matter. Literary influence is a secondary business. What is important is the standpoint, which is the key to any critical judgment of

5 *Ibid.*, I, 125–29; II, 24.

Orwell. It is easy to say that *Down and Out in Paris and London* is better than *A Clergyman's Daughter*, but this ought not to be reduced to the plausible generalization that he is a better "observer" than "novelist." The real problem lies deeper, in the available conceptions of "the novel."

"Telling a story straightforwardly and without frills." "Story," after all, is the whole question. Maugham is the characteristic Edwardian "storyteller": that is to say, the collector and retailer of human episodes. Orwell had the material for this (it is usually collected at a distance and in other lands), but only his first novel, *Burmese Days*, is at all of its kind. Even there, while the plot concerns personal intrigue among an isolated European group on an Eastern station, the stress is on the complicated social consequences of imperialism and within this there is what we can now recognize as the deep Orwell pattern; the man who tries to break from the standards of his group but who is drawn back into it and, in this case, destroyed. What is unique about the novel in Orwell's work is that he creates an entire social and physical milieu within which the social criticism and the personal break are defined elements. In all his later novels, the essential form is shaped by what became separated elements: the personal break, and social criticism through it, in the novels of the 1930s; the social criticism, with the personal break inside it, in *Nineteen Eighty-four*.

That seems a clear development, but it omits the material of "observation." Having found one form for this, in the journal of *Down and Out in Paris and London*, Orwell clearly wanted to incorporate it in a novel. This is the developmental significance of *A Clergyman's Daughter*, where the direct observation and the fiction are unusually close. But from then on he seems to have accepted the division between "documentary" and "fiction." A possible reshaping of the novel was evaded, or proved too difficult: not, I would say, because he was "not really a novelist" but because a problem of consciousness, which he shared with other writers of his time, emerged as a problem of form.

For Orwell the interest of Joyce had been his direct realization of "ordinary" experience. It is Bloom he selects from *Ulysses*: that recording "inside" and "outside" the ordinary man. But this description conceals the problem of the relationship of the novelist to his character, which is always a form of relationship of the writer to his world. And the relationship that matters here can be alternatively described as "acceptance" or "passivity." It is an impersonal form, the logical consequence of James's emphasis on the artist's "handling" of "matter." It is "the artist refined out of existence," observing, recording. Except that in practice it is impossible to observe anything without being in some relationship to it. The apparent relationship, that which is recommended and publicized, is the "aesthetic"; the "handling" of the matter, the preoccupation with words, that is Joyce's actual development. But the "matter" can only be handled in this way—can only be abstracted, stay still to be "written" —if a particular relationship is in fact assumed. "Acceptance" or "passivity": the difference between the positive and negative descriptions is less important than the fact of the relationship itself—a refraining from intervention,

or, more, a seeing no need to intervene, since the avail-
ability of the "matter" is the artist's primary and only
concern.

Orwell's artistic failure in his novels of the 1930s is in
a way, and paradoxically, due to his social achievement.
He had known passivity, at least, very closely, as he describes in *Down and Out in Paris and London*. But he
had known it not in his capacity as a writer but as a vic-
tim. We have seen him describe as an "invasion" the
growth of that social consciousness that required his intervention, that made either acceptance or passivity impossible (though he went back to the idea of acceptance
and passivity in "Inside the Whale," at a time when
the social intervention could be held to have failed).

Then, in shaping a literary form, he created the figure
of the intermediary (the "shock-absorber of the bourgeoisie," as he had referred to people like himself) who
goes around and to whom things happen. This figure is
not Orwell, though it has Orwell's experiences, in *A
Clergyman's Daughter* and then in a different way in
Keep the Aspidistra Flying. The figure is passive; things
happen *to* Dorothy, or *to* Comstock. And this pattern
releases one element of Orwell's experience—the things
that had "happened" to him—but not (or only partly)
why they had happened, not the intervening or "invad-
ing" consciousness. Dorothy, certainly, is the more passive figure. Comstock, in *Keep the Aspidistra Flying*, is
given some of Orwell's whole consciousness: he not only
tries to live without money but declares war on money
and its system. Comstock is an active and critical figure
in all the initial exploration, but increasingly there is a
contradiction within the mode of observation. The active

and resourceful persistence of Orwell, the impressive survival and remaking of an active self, is steadily cut out, as the accepting observation continues. What begins as a protest becomes a whine, and the reabsorption of Comstock into a world of manipulable objects is accomplished with a kind of perverse triumph; the "character" of the intermediary (like the "character" of Flory or of Dorothy) becomes the "justification" of the eventual submission or defeat.

This is the strange transmutation of "acceptance," or "passivity." In Orwell, because of his uncertainties, it is neither an artistic discipline nor an acceptable worldview. His final attempt at a Bloom figure is Bowling in *Coming Up for Air*, written at a recollecting and abstracting distance and perhaps for that reason more consistent internally. Bowling breaks from an orthodox routine, like the others, though not into exposure, where things happen to him, but instead into the past, an old England and his childhood; and then the experience is of loss, disillusion, disenchantment. *Coming Up for Air* came after Orwell's crucial political experience in Spain and its consequences, which we shall have to look at in detail. But elements of the literary decision are continuous: observation through a limited intermediary, with the limit being the basis for a deeper pattern: a self-proving of both the need and the impossibility of a sustained break, with active intervention dwindling to a temporary protest or self-assertion. The significance of this pattern in the altered world of *Nineteen Eighty-four* will need further analysis, when the other changes have been taken into account.

Having failed to solve his profoundly difficult problem

in the novel, Orwell turned to other forms that were in practice more available. His social and political writing was a direct release of consciousness, the practical consequence of intervention. "Shooting an Elephant," for example, is more successful than anything in *Burmese Days* not because it is "documentary" rather than fiction—the fiction, as we have seen, similarly relied on things that had happened to him—but because instead of a Flory an Orwell is present: a successfully created character in every real sense. Instead of diluting his consciousness through an intermediary, as the mode of fiction had seemed to require, he now writes directly and powerfully about his whole experience. The prose is at once strengthened, as the alternation between an anxious impersonation and a passively impersonal observation gives way to a direct voice in which there is more literary creation than in all the more conventionally "imaginative" attempts. "Shooting an Elephant" is not a document; it is a literary work. The distinction between "fiction" and "nonfiction" is not a matter of whether the experience happened to the writer, not a distinction between "real" and "imaginary." The distinction is one of range and consciousness. Written human experience of an unspecialized and primary kind must always be recognized as literature. Particular forms, and the origins of the material, are secondary questions. Orwell began to write literature, in the full sense, when he found this nonfictional form capable of realizing his experience directly.

Realizing *his* experience—not only what had happened to him and what he had observed, but what he felt about it and what he thought about it, the self-definition of "Orwell," the man inside and outside the experience.

Perhaps the best example is *The Road to Wigan Pier*. As it happens Orwell's diary notes for this book have been published.[6] A comparison of the diary and the book is interesting, for a number of reasons. It is easy enough to find in the notes the sources of many of the descriptions: of the Brookers' lodging house, for example, in the opening chapter. But what is also evident, comparing the two, is the literary process. There is the expected and necessary development of a scene in the published version, a fuller and more fluent description, details recollected from memory. But there is also a saturation of the scene with feeling. Orwell is present and responding, indeed directing response, as he is only there toward the end in the diary notes. He seems also to have shifted the lodgers around a bit: Joe, at the Brookers', is described in the notes as a lodger at a previous house—a house that is not in the book. So in the book the Brookers' house is not only given the emphasis of first place but treated as a first, representative experience ("it struck me that this place must be fairly normal as lodging-houses in the industrial areas go") when in the diary there is a preceding and rather different experience.

This is just one small example to illustrate the point about "documentary" experience. The writer shapes and organizes what happened to produce a particular effect, based on experience but then created out of it. The overall organization of *The Road to Wigan Pier* is a major example. In the first part, the "observation" of the industrial North, one of the key points, in literary terms, is that Orwell is the isolated observer going around and seeing for himself. This created character is then used

6 *Ibid.*, I, 170–214.

to important effect in the second half, the argument about socialism, where he is contrasted with the jargon-ridden bourgeois socialists: "The first thing that must strike any outside observer is that Socialism in its developed form is a theory confined entirely to the middle class."[7]

The external political point is not what is most important here: "in its developed form" is an infinitely saving clause. The key point is the persona, the "outside observer"—that is, Orwell. An essential link between the two parts is indeed this character: "inside" and then "outside" the experience.

We learn from the diary notes that after some days of wandering on his own through the Midlands, Orwell was given some political contacts in Lancashire and met working-class socialists and members of the Unemployed Workers' Movement. Through one of these contacts he got the chance to go down a mine; and through the collectors he obtained facts about housing conditions. It is important that he omits most of this experience—an actual social and political network—in *The Road to Wigan Pier*. Even in the diary, some of the difficulties are apparent. A local trade-union official and his wife, "both . . . working-class people," are seen as living (in a twelve- or fourteen-shilling-a-week estate house) in an "entirely middle-class" atmosphere. Orwell has his own definition of what the working class is like. That is, presumably, why he could say, after meeting these people (who had embarrassed him by calling him "comrade") and "an electrician who takes a prominent part in the Socialist movement," that "socialism" was a middle-class affair. If

[7] *The Road to Wigan Pier*, p. 173.

a workingman is a socialist he is already, presumably, middle class, the character of the working class being already known.

But here the political point *is* the literary point. What is created in the book is an isolated independent observer and the objects of his observation. Intermediate characters and experiences that do not form part of this world— this structure of feeling—are simply omitted. What is left in is "documentary" enough, but the process of selection and organization is a literary act: the character of the observer is as real and yet created as the real and yet created world he so powerfully describes.

All of Orwell's writing until 1937 is, then, a series of works and experiments around a common problem. Instead of dividing them into "fiction" and "documentaries" we should see them as sketches toward the creation of his most successful character, "Orwell." This would not be so successful if it had not been so intensely and painfully lived. The exposure to poverty and suffering and filth and waste was as real as it was deliberate, and the record of the exposure is a remarkable enlargement of our literature. But in and through the exposure a character is being created, who is real in the precise sense that he becomes this writer, this shaping presence. Flory and Dorothy and Comstock, or the later Bowling, are aspects of this character but without his centrality. The only literary form that can contain the full character at this stage is the "non-fiction journal" of an isolated writer exposed to a suffering but unconnecting world. The need to intervene, to force active connections, is the road away from Wigan Pier, back to an indifferent and sleepy and uncaring world, which has to be told about the isolation and the suffering.

At just this point, between the diary and the book, the Spanish war broke out. The writing, and the character, moved into a different dimension.

Politics

V

Orwell's original intention in going to Spain
was to "gather material for newspaper articles
etc."[1] But he was told that to get into Spain he
needed papers from some organization of the
Left. Victor Gollancz had started the Left Book
Club in May 1936; its selection committee con-
sisted of Gollancz, Harold Laski, and John
Strachey. *The Road to Wigan Pier* was to be
published in March 1937 by the Left Book Club,
though with a cautionary note. It was through
Strachey that Orwell made his first attempt to
get papers for Spain, going with an introduction
to Harry Pollitt of the Communist Party, who
asked if he would undertake to join the International Brigade. Orwell replied that he could not
undertake to join anything until he had seen
what was happening. He then made contact

[1] *Collected Essays*, . . . , I, 316.

with the Independent Labour Party, with whom previously he had had "some slight connection," and was given a letter of introduction to John McNair in Barcelona. It was mainly because of this letter that when he decided to fight he joined the militia of the POUM, with which the ILP had connections. As it happened, joining the POUM militia pushed him into the center of an intricate and bitter political struggle between rival socialist groups. But as we can see from the way things went, and in particular from his original approach through Strachey to Pollitt, this was in no way of his own seeking. He had been critical of what he knew as Marxist theory, of its jargon and its sectarian and factional feuds, before he left England. As he argued in *The Road to Wigan Pier*, the urgent duty of socialists—to make more people act like socialists—was being hindered by what seemed to him an alienated atmosphere and style. He thought of himself as an anti-imperialist and an antifascist, as a believer in equality, and only through these positions as a socialist. Joining the militia of the POUM was not an affiliation in the conventional political sense. What he had criticized among socialists and Marxists in Britain he found in the POUM as much as in the Communist Party in Spain. But it was the readiest way in which he could fight against the fascists, and at first the doctrinal differences hardly mattered to him. Some months later, when he knew much more about them, he took the same attitude when he wanted to go to fight in Madrid, asking for a recommendation from a friend in the Communist Party. For still, as he said, fighting where he could be most useful was his primary concern; the shades of political doctrine were at best secondary. Indeed, "as far as my purely personal preferences went I would have liked to join the Anarchists," but serving on the most critical front came first.

These details are important, both for the record (which has become very confused) and for the clear impression they give of Orwell's undoctrinal socialism. It can indeed be argued that socialism as such was always secondary, in his mind, to the struggle against fascism and imperialism and inequality. Socialism was a general idea, a general name, against all these evils, and before he left England it had little more positive content. The experience of revolutionary Barcelona determined him to fight, rather than any positive affiliation conceived in Britain. It was the first time he had ever been "in a town where the working class was in the saddle."[2] His "vague idea of fighting if it seemed worthwhile" was transformed by this new experience, and joining the militia to fight the fascists "seemed the only conceivable thing to do." In the militia "many of the normal motives of civilized life—snobbishness, money-grubbing, fear of the boss, etc. —had simply ceased to exist. The ordinary class-division of society had disappeared to an extent that is almost unthinkable in the money-tainted air of England."[3]

The experience was, in a true sense, a political breakthrough:

One had been in a community where hope was more normal than apathy or cynicism, where the word "comrade" stood for comradeship and not, as in most countries, for humbug. . . . In that community where no one was on the make, where there was a shortage

[2] *Homage to Catalonia*, p. 8.
[3] *Ibid.*, p. 102.

of everything but no privilege and no bootlicking, one got, perhaps, a crude foretaste of what the opening stages of Socialism might be like. And, after all, instead of disillusioning me it deeply attracted me. The effect was to make my desire to see Socialism established much more actual than it had been before.[4]

Or, as he put it even more strongly in a letter of June 1937, when he was preparing to leave Spain, "I have seen wonderful things and at last really believe in Socialism, which I never did before."[5]

This emphasis is crucial. During those months in Spain Orwell became a revolutionary socialist. Up to a point there is a clear line from his experience in the years of poverty, exposure, and rejection of privilege—the wandering years—to the experience of shared hardship in Barcelona. But there is also a clear break from a personal option to a common cause. What had been mainly a passive exposure to the worst kinds of hardship became an active involvement in the struggle to end them. It is ironic that at the moment when Orwell became a revolutionary socialist he became involved with an internal struggle so deep and permanent that it is still very difficult to see his experience and his development clearly.

While he was at the front in the early months of 1937 he listened to endless arguments about the future of the war and the revolution. The situation was indeed so complicated that there was virtually no limit to argument. In broad outline, it was said on one hand that everything must be subordinated to the duty of defeating the fascist armies, and on the other hand that fascism could be de-

[4] *Ibid.*, pp. 102–103.
[5] *Collected Essays, . . . ,* I, 269.

feated only if there was a simultaneous social revolution. In subsequent historical accounts, these cases have been repeated and examined, in great detail and often with bitterness. To move in that area at all is like moving in a minefield. Most historians have taken the view that the revolution—mainly anarcho-syndicalist but with the POUM taking part—was an irrelevant distraction from a desperate war. Some, at the time and after, have gone so far as to describe it as deliberate sabotage of the war effort. Only a few have argued on the other side that the suppression of the revolution by the main body of Republican forces was an act of power politics related to Soviet policy that amounted to a betrayal of the cause for which the Spanish people were fighting.

As we have seen, the experience of revolutionary Barcelona made Orwell a militant socialist. But in the chaos and inactivity of the early months at the front, he usually supported the communist line. It seemed to him a matter of practical common sense that there should be unity and efficiency; indeed, echoes of his own early training as an officer cadet and in the Imperial Police can be heard again and again as he describes the disorganization of the revolutionary militia. At the same time, his experience of its revolutionary spirit, its practical comradeship, was paramount. This, before everything, was why he was fighting at all.

It is difficult to say how this conflict would have resolved itself if the situation had not changed. The contrary impulses in Orwell's mind were only too clearly reflected in the immediate pressures. From his education and training he believed in efficiency as an isolated value. From his social development during the wandering years in England he had come to believe, profoundly, in the common cause of the oppressed, and he was impatient of political divisions that delayed or prevented its expression. In both these respects he was a natural Popular Front man, and the official Republican arguments impressed him. But his previously passive belief in a common cause had been realized and released by the revolutionary experience: the sense of living in a new human world. When he went back to Barcelona after three-and-a-half months at the front, he found a different city. In December 1936 it had been a place "where class distinctions and great differences of wealth hardly existed." Now "things were returning to normal. The smart restaurants and hotels were full of rich people wolfing expensive meals, while for the working-class population food-prices had jumped enormously without any corresponding rise in wages."[6] The revolutionary atmosphere was disappearing, in almost every respect, and the working class no longer even seemed to be in control. This was not only the result of political changes, leading to the end of the popular militia and the reorganization of a centralized army and administration. But when the power struggle, implicit in these changes, erupted in what looked now like a "normal" city, Orwell's sympathies would not have been in doubt, quite apart from the fact that having served in the POUM militia he was part of the movement that was declared illegal and suppressed. His account of that fighting brings out its extraordinary complexity, and he is quick to say that he can only report what he saw and that like every other account his own is partisan and subject to bias and error. But what happened to him and his

[6] *Homage to Catalonia*, p. 110.

comrades from the front was so arbitrary and brutal that his choice of action was inevitable. Different accounts were given, and are still given, of the start of the street fighting and of its political motives. All Orwell knew, and could know, was that the ragged men back from the front, in this again class-divided city, were being rounded up by guards and police in the name of the struggle against fascism, and, most accounts say, in the name of the true cause of socialism and of the people. The experience left a scar that was never likely to heal. One would think worse of him, indeed, if it had ever healed.

Homage to Catalonia is in some ways Orwell's most important and most moving book. It is an unforgettably vivid personal account of a revolution and a civil war. But it has been less highly valued than some of his earlier and later writing for political reasons of a double kind. His inevitably controversial accounts of the internal struggles have cut the book off, then and since, from many readers on the Left. But also, and less often noted, his open and moving commitment to revolutionary socialism has cut the book off from a different and much larger group of readers, who from his later work have a fixed idea of Orwell as the voice of political disillusion, of the inevitable failure of revolution and of socialism. There is material for this view in *Homage to Catalonia*, in the account of the loss and suppression of the revolutionary spirit: "it was simply a temporary and local phase in an enormous game that is being played over the whole surface of the earth."[7]

Yet in none of his writing about Spain does Orwell draw what can later be seen as the right-wing conclusion.

[7] *Ibid.*, p. 102.

Though the revolutionary movement to which he belonged had been suppressed, he returned from Spain a convinced revolutionary socialist: "when I see an actual flesh-and-blood worker in conflict with his natural enemy, the policeman, I do not have to ask myself which side I am on."[8] He was certainly suspicious, as he had been before he went, of what he called "bourgeois communism," with its idealized "worker." But in the actual conflict he had made his choice. He was very bitter about official communist policy in Spain, and about the foreign reporting of the Spanish struggle. This hatred of what he was already calling "Stalinism" never left him. But his position after the Spanish experience is that of a revolutionary socialist: what would now, from the outside, be called an "ultra." His account of the Spanish struggle is very similar to later accounts of the struggles in Budapest or in Paris; written from a revolutionary socialist position, it is bitterly hostile at once to the capitalist order and to orthodox communism. This stage of Orwell's political development needs exceptional emphasis.

It is perhaps of even greater interest to see how and when Orwell moved from this position to the position of his last years. For example, when he wrote "Looking Back on the Spanish War," in 1942 and long after his controversies with what he saw as the official lies of the communist press, it was still fascism that he saw as the totalitarian danger. It was fascist propaganda, and such pro-Franco propaganda as that of the *Daily Mail* and the *Catholic Herald*, which led him to reflect that "the very concept of objective truth is fading out of the world."[9]

[8] *Ibid.*, p. 119.
[9] *Collected Essays, . . . ,* II, 258.

And it was from Nazi theory that he drew the concept of "a nightmare world in which the Leader, or some ruling clique, controls not only the future but the *past*. If the Leader says of such and such an event, 'It never happened'—well, it never happened. If he says that two and two are five—well, two and two are five."[10] These direct anticipations of *Nineteen Eighty-four* are primarily responses to fascism, and the "re-institution of slavery," which he also sees happening, is based on the Nazi labor camps. Nothing could be more false than the quite general idea that Orwell returned from Spain a disillusioned socialist, who then gave his energy to warnings against a totalitarian socialist future.

Yet tracing the real development is difficult. In 1938 Orwell joined the Independent Labour Party and explained; "One has got to be actively a Socialist, not merely sympathetic to Socialism, or one plays into the hands of our always active enemies."[11] He said that "for perhaps ten years past" he had had "some grasp of the real nature of capitalist society" and that while he hoped the Labour Party would win the next election, he had no illusions about its socialism and did not intend to be "led up the garden path in the name of capitalist democracy."

Again in 1938, he defended the antiwar movement from the implication that pacifism was a soft option for intellectuals:

The truth is that any real advance, let alone any genuinely revolutionary change, can only begin when the mass of the people definitely refuse capitalist-imperialist war. . . . So long as they show them-

[10] *Ibid.*, p. 259.
[11] *Ibid.*, I, 337–38.

selves willing to fight "in defence of democracy", or "against Fascism", or for any other flyblown slogan, the same trick will be played upon them again and again.[12]

Reviewing Borkenau's *The Communist International* he wrote:

> If the problems of western capitalism are to be solved, it will have to be through a third alternative, a movement which is genuinely revolutionary, i.e. willing to make drastic changes and to use violence if necessary, but which does not lose touch, as Communism and Fascism have done, with the essential values of democracy. Such a thing is by no means unthinkable. The germs of such a movement exist in several countries, and they are capable of growing.[13]

In January 1939 he wrote to Herbert Read:

> I believe it is vitally necessary for those of us who intend to oppose the coming war to start organising for illegal anti-war activities . . . I quite agree that people, especially people who have any kind of notoriety, can get the best results by fighting in the open, but we might find it extremely useful to have an underground organisation *as well*.[14]

In this and a further letter to Read he made practical suggestions for underground activity, in a political situation in which most of the Left would have compromised and in which the "dissident lefts like ourselves" would be the only alternative opposition to the fascists. In July 1939, writing about British imperialism, he asked, "What meaning would there be, even if it were successful, in bring-

[12] *Ibid.*, p. 331.
[13] *Ibid.*, p. 350.
[14] *Ibid.*, pp. 377–78.

ing down Hitler's system in order to stabilise something that is far bigger and in its different way just as bad?"[15]

It is worth adding that during this period of revolutionary antiwar socialism, Orwell was not, in the jargon he so frequently criticized, a "Trotskyite." He often argued that this description was simply loose abuse, though he used "Stalinist" himself. But he made it clear that in his view the faults of the Soviet Union went back to "the aims and nature of the Bolshevik Party": "Trotsky, in exile, denounces the Russian dictatorship, but he is probably as much responsible for it as any man now living."[16] Attempting a new definition of revolutionary socialism, Orwell found no effective organizational home, although he continued to hope and plan for one.

Then came the change—almost overnight, as it seems. It was not simply a reaction to the beginning of the war, or even to the Stalin-Hitler agreement. Indeed,

> the night before the Russo-German pact was announced I dreamed that the war had started. It was one of those dreams which, whatever Freudian inner meaning they may have, do sometimes reveal to you the true state of your feelings. It taught me two things, first, that I should be simply relieved when the long-dreaded war started, secondly, that I was patriotic at heart, would not sabotage or act against my own side, would support the war, would fight in it if possible.[17]

He had been back in England since late March. His father had died in June. In the essay from which the account of the dream comes, "My Country Right or Left,"

[15] *Ibid.*, p. 397.
[16] *Ibid.*, p. 381.
[17] *Ibid.*, p. 539.

he spoke of growing up too young for the 1914–1918 war, and "you felt yourself a little less than a man, because you had missed it." He had had frequent military training, since childhood and the cadet corps, and "part of the fascination that the Spanish civil war had for people of about my age was that it was so like the Great War." Reviewing Muggeridge's *The Thirties* in the following spring, he wrote:

> It is the emotion of the middle-class man, brought up in the military tradition, who finds in the moment of crisis that he is a patriot after all. It is all very well to be "advanced" or "enlightened", to snigger at Colonel Blimp and proclaim your emancipation from all traditional loyalties, but a time comes when the sand of the desert is sodden red and what have I done for thee, England, my England? As I was brought up in this tradition myself I can recognise it under strange disguises, and also sympathise with it, for even at its stupidest and most sentimental it is a comelier thing than the shallow self-righteousness of the left-wing intelligentsia.[18]

On this explanation, Orwell's abrupt change is simply a reversion to type. And in a sense this is true. But under the simple readjustment, which was traditionally available, a more profound process of discouragement had been occurring. This is (following *Coming Up for Air*) directly indicated in "Inside the Whale," written during the summer of 1939, when in relation to Henry Miller he writes sympathetically of passivity:

> the viewpoint of a man who believes the world-process to be outside his control and who in any case hardly wishes to control it. . . . Progress and reaction have

18 *Ibid.*, p. 535.

both turned out to be swindles. Seemingly there is nothing left but quietism—robbing reality of its terrors by simply submitting to it. Get inside the whale —or rather, admit that you are inside it (for you *are*, of course). Give yourself over to the world-process, stop fighting against it or pretending that you control it; simply accept it, endure it, record it.[19]

This is his prescription for a writer under the dangers of his time, but in a more general way it marks his real discouragement. He had exposed himself to so much hardship and then fought so hard; had got a bullet in the throat in Spain; had been severely ill with a tubercular lesion; had given so much of his energy to what seemed a desert of political illusions, lies, and bad faith. Between the myth of "England" and this profound European disillusion he had to make what settlement he could find.

This is the right way, I think, to follow his subsequent political development. Much of Orwell's wartime journalism is lively, but it is not his best work. In his criticism of people who went on holding or who came to hold positions identical or close to his own between 1937 and 1939, there is some lively polemic but also a good deal of rancor and even random abuse. Under the desperate pressures of the time, as he had reason to know as well as anyone, it was hardly possible to find any decent and consistent position, and the sectarian squabbling, the branding and naming of "defeatist" groups, had a smallness and meanness that at times he recognized. In his diary of April 27, 1942, he noted: "We are all drowning in filth. When I talk to anyone or read the writings of

19 *Ibid.*, pp. 519, 526.

anyone who has any axe to grind, I feel that intellectual honesty and balanced judgment have simply disappeared from the face of the earth. Everyone's thought is forensic. . . ."[20] Yet this is as true, it seems to me, of his own wartime articles as of those he criticized—but not wholly true. There is hysterical overstatement in the very face of overstatement and hysteria. At a public level, apart from his attacks on "defeatists," and apart from his work at the BBC—where he genuinely tried to keep the propaganda to India "decent"—he attempted for some time to combine support for the war with a program of turning it into a revolutionary war that would defeat Hitler and the English class system simultaneously. It was a hope like any other, but the characteristic Orwell note returns when in late 1944 he publicly reviewed all the errors of analysis he had made through these years and concluded, "Whether we 'opposed' the war or 'supported' it, I think the first admission we ought to make is that *we were all wrong*."[21] It is at one level a reasonable admission, characteristic of Orwell's profound honesty and frankness. But at another level it introduces an element that was to combine with the more submerged despairs: the notion that all political thinking, or almost all, was a mode of adjustment to one's own wishes and fantasies. As he wrote in 1946:

It is not easy to believe in the survival of civilization. . . . I think one must continue the political struggle, just as a doctor must try to save the life of a patient who is probably going to die. But . . . we shall get nowhere unless we start by recognising that political

[20] *Ibid.*, II, 423.
[21] *Ibid.*, III, 294.

behaviour is largely non-rational, that the world is suffering from some kind of mental disease which must be diagnosed before it can be cured.[22]

This is the conclusion that matters in understanding his last work. Certainly it was given a political super-structure, the key element of which was the substitution of communism for fascism as the totalitarian threat. This was part of the movement of the times, in the early years of the Cold War. But given Orwell's experience and development, it was crucial. He saw the atomic bomb as a major turning point: "either we renounce it or it destroys us" (November 1945).[23] But the political shapes were altering. In 1943 he had written:

The dreary world which the American millionaires and their British hangers-on intend to impose on us begins to take shape. The British people, in the mass, don't want such a world. . . . Sentimentally, the majority of people in this country would rather be in a tie-up with Russia than with America.[24]

By late 1947 this was reversed:

"If you had to choose between Russia and America, which would you choose?" . . . We are no longer strong enough to stand alone, and if we fail to bring a western European union into being, we shall be obliged, in the long run, to subordinate our policy to that of one Great Power or the other. And in spite of all the fashionable chatter of the moment, every-one knows in his heart that we should choose America.[25]

[22] *Ibid.*, IV, 249.
[23] *Ibid.*, 19.
[24] *Ibid.*, II, 282.
[25] *Ibid.*, IV, 398.

Beneath these political adjustments was the deeper fear that the world would fall apart into two or three superstates, each holding the atomic bomb, and that within each such state there would be a new authoritarianism: what he came to call, in a phrase taken from Borkenau, "oligarchical collectivism." This is, of course, the world of *Nineteen Eighty-four*, but it is significant that in just these critical years Orwell diagnosed a future based on power politics, the permanent war economy, and authoritarianism—trends that he saw everywhere, behind almost all the political labels—and then identified it, directly, only with the Soviet system. He remained a democratic socialist. He gave most of his political energies to the defense of civil liberties over a wide front. But in his deepest vision of what was to come, he had at once actualized a general nightmare and then, in the political currents of the time, narrowed its reference until the nightmare itself became one of its own shaping elements.

Projections

•

VI

Orwell began writing *Animal Farm* in November 1943. It was completed three months later. Several publishers rejected it, some on political grounds. It is ironic that a book written against the grain of prevailing public opinion should have appeared, eighteen months later, at a time when the political situation had changed and it could be used, eagerly, in what was becoming the Cold War.

For a long time the book was inseparable from that ironic political context. Orwell was described on the Left as having run "shrieking into the arms of the capitalist publishers" (*Marxist Quarterly*, January 1956), which was certainly not how it felt to him at the time ("I am having hell and all to find a publisher for it here though normally I have no difficulty in publishing my stuff"). At the same time, the book was undoubtedly used by people whom Orwell had no sympathy with, and when followed by *Nineteen Eighty-four*, which was even more extensively used, it fixed a version of Orwell that he, at least, would have considered misleading. The whole story of the refusal and then the promotion of *Animal Farm* is full of ironies of the kind Orwell was now directly concerned with, including the episode of the special edition for Ukrainian refugees of which nearly half was seized by the American authorities in Germany and handed over to Soviet officials.[1]

Animal Farm is unique in Orwell's writing by the absence of an Orwell figure. It is in this sense a more complete projection of his way of seeing the world than anything else he wrote. Yet the terms of the projection limited the consciousness with which the Orwell figure had been invented to deal. It is a work of simplification, in both the good and bad senses.

Orwell described it once as a squib, but it was always more serious than that. He wrote in the preface to the Ukrainian edition:

> Nothing has contributed so much to the corruption of the original idea of Socialism as the belief that Russia is a Socialist country and that every act of its rulers must be excused, if not imitated. And so for the past ten years I have been convinced that the destruction of the Soviet myth was essential if we wanted a revival of the Socialist movement. On my return from Spain I thought of exposing the Soviet myth in a story that could be easily understood by almost anyone and which could be easily translated into other languages.[2]

[1] *Collected Essays, . . . ,* IV, 379.
[2] *Ibid.,* III, 404–406.

The precision of his political aim, and yet the search for simplicity and generality, carry some inevitable contradictions. More important, perhaps, is Orwell's emphasis on the destruction of the myth of Soviet society, which he believed was common among the Left in the West. Perhaps that intention, at some stage, was paramount. For in the same preface he goes so far as to say:

> Even if I had the power, I would not wish to interfere in Soviet domestic affairs; I would not condemn Stalin and his associates merely for their barbaric and undemocratic methods. It is quite possible that, even with the best intentions, they could not have acted otherwise under the conditions prevailing there.

But not only did no recognition of that kind appear in the work itself; it could not have appeared, given its stress on actual conditions and on a particular historical situation, in any work conceived and executed as a general fable. Indeed, by the time the specific situation had been so generally translated, it was always possible, even likely, that not only the myth of Soviet socialism, but also the myth of revolution, would in fact be "destroyed."

Certainly *Animal Farm* has been widely interpreted in this way. Orwell is produced as "evidence" against a new revolutionary generation. The revival of the socialist movement, which he said he wanted, is met by the sad ghost of his late imagination. Perhaps this was inevitable in the exploitation of literature by the politics of the Cold War. But something deeper has to be faced: the real consciousness of the fable itself. Past the easy exploitation and the equally easy rejection, the fable in *Animal Farm* offers positive and negative evidence of a permanently interesting kind.

Orwell got the germ of the fable from seeing

> a little boy, perhaps ten years old, driving a huge
> cart-horse along a narrow path, whipping it whenever
> it tried to turn. It struck me that if only such animals
> became aware of their strength we should have no
> power over them, and that men exploit animals in
> much the same way as the rich exploit the pro-
> letariat.[3]

This insight is already of a rather different kind from the
eventual projection. The speed of his figurative transition
from animals to the proletariat is interesting, showing as
it does a residue of thinking of the poor as animals, powerful but stupid. Men, of course, here and in the story, are
seen as exploiters. And the worst thing about the Bolshevik pigs, in the story, is that they become indistin-
guishable from drunken, greedy, and cruel men. The no-
ble beast is the workhorse Boxer.

It is worth considering this alongside Orwell's remarks
on Swift's Houyhnhnms and Yahoos.[4] He is quick to
diagnose Swift's disgust with man and apparent preference for animals, but he goes on to say that actually the
Houyhnhnms, whom he finds unattractive, are more like
men than the Yahoos, who are a deliberate degradation.
Very complicated feelings are involved here. The powerful but stupid horses of *Animal Farm* are looked on with
great respect and pity. The men and the pigs are intelligent, calculating, greedy, and cruel. This is surely more
than a simple operative analogy. It is a substantial, even
physical, response.

The other element of the analogy is exploitation. If

[3] *Ibid.*, p. 406.
[4] *Ibid.*, IV, 217–19.

they became aware of their strength, *we* should have no power over them. Orwell here is thinking about some-thing mcre than a political event, about a range of re-lations in man's use of animals and of nature. The point he goes on to is in any other terms very surprising:

> I proceeded to analyse Marx's theory from the ani-mals' point of view. To them it was clear that the concept of a class struggle between humans was pure illusion, since whenever it was necessary to exploit animals, all humans united against them: the true struggle is between animals and humans. From this point of departure, it was not difficult to elaborate the story.[5]

The true struggle between animals and humans: is that the real theme of *Animal Farm*? It is difficult to say so, without most of the surface of the story collapsing. What really happens, I think, is that the very deep identifica-tion between the laboring and exploited animals and the laboring and exploited poor is retained, almost unnoticed, as a base for the exposure of that "pure illusion . . . of a class struggle between humans"—humans, now, being capitalists and revolutionaries, the old ruling class and the new, who, whatever their differences and their con-flicts, can be depended upon to go on exploiting the crea-tures on whose backs they live, and even, as at the end of the story, to unite against them. Orwell is opposing here more than the Soviet or Stalinist experience. Both the consciousness of the workers and the possibility of au-thentic revolution are denied.

These denials, I would say, are inhuman. But it is part of the paradox of Orwell that from this despairing base he

[5] *Ibid.*, III, 406.

is able to generate an immediate and practical humanity: the comradeship of the suffering, which he feels very deeply, and also, more actively, the critical skepticism of the exploited, an unexpected kind of consciousness that informs the story. I have said that *Animal Farm* is unique among Orwell's books because it contains no Orwell figure, no isolated man who breaks from conformity but is then defeated and reabsorbed. This figure is, rather, projected into a collective action: this is what happens to the animals who free themselves and then, through violence and fraud, are again enslaved.

The collective projection has a further effect. What happens is a common rather than an isolated experience, for all its bitterness; and the whine of ragged nerves, the despair of a lonely trajectory are replaced by an actively communicative tone in the critical narrative. A paradoxical confidence, an assured and active and laughing intelligence, is manifested in the very penetration and exposure of the experience of defeat. Through this mode, Orwell is able to release an exceptionally strong and pure prose. "All animals are equal . . . but some are more equal than others." It is not surprising that this phrase has passed into ordinary language with a meaning much stronger than that of simple satire on revolutionary betrayal. It is one of those permanent statements about the gap between pretense and actuality, profession and practice, that covers a very wide range. In many places throughout *Animal Farm*, this strong and liberating intelligence transforms a bitter perception into an active and stimulating critique. Beyond the details of the local analogy, and paradoxically beyond the more fundamental despair, this lively awareness connects and informs. Even the last sad scene, where the excluded animals look from man to pig and pig to man and cannot tell which is which, carries a feeling that is more than disillusion and defeat. Seeing that they are the same because they act the same, never mind the labels and the formalities—that is a moment of gained consciousness, a potentially liberating discovery. In its small scale and within its limited terms, *Animal Farm* has a radical energy that goes far beyond its occasion and has its own kind of permanence.

Nineteen Eighty-four is obviously very different. The curve of isolated feeling, of a ragged and breathless exposure, has returned and is decisive. Yet there are still many elements that belong to a more liberating consciousness. The appendix, "The Principles of Newspeak," was never fully incorporated in the imaginative world, but its central perception of a relation between linguistic and social forms is powerful: "the special function of certain Newspeak words, of which *oldthink* was one, was not so much to express meanings as to destroy them."[6] Some Newspeak words—*prolefeed, speedwise, sexcrime* —have already, a generation later, an ominously familiar sound. So too have the names of new government departments: in Newspeak, Minipax, Miniluv and Miniplenty, I would expect that the copywriters of Mintech are admirers of Orwell, but if they have read him they have certainly not understood him. Much of the jargon of "modernization"—that extraordinary substitute for social democracy that the British Labour government adopted and propagated in the 1960s—is almost wholly Newspeak. Some of the techniques of news management sound similarly familiar. The Fiction Department, as an

[6] *Nineteen Eighty-four*, p. 311.

institution, would now hardly even be noticed. And when Winston Smith describes a typical film show—"the helicopter planted a 20 kilo bomb in among them terrific flash and the boat went all to matchwood. Then there was a wonderful shot of a child's arm going up up up right up into the air a helicopter with a camera in its nose must have followed it up"—it is as if he had seen the television newsreels from Vietnam; only the weight of the bomb is an absurd underestimate.

Again, in a rather different way, "Big Brother Is Watching You" has also made its way into ordinary language, as the motto of a skeptical resistance. In these very simple and powerful ways Orwell succeeded in articulating certain quite evident elements of our prolonged social crisis. As an intransigent enemy of every kind of *thoughtcrime* and *doublethink*, Orwell is still close and alive.

His vision of power politics is also close and convincing. The transposition of official "allies" and "enemies" has happened, almost openly, in the generation since he wrote. His idea of a world divided into three blocs— Oceania, Eurasia, and Eastasia, of which two are always at war with the third though the alliances change—is again too close for comfort. And there are times when one can believe that what "had been called England or Britain" has become simply Airstrip One.

With these elements of the projection so recognizable, at least in their general outlines, it is necessary to ask why so much else is so wrong. It is significant that Orwell took his model of a controlled and military society from Soviet communism, even including detailed elements of its past such as the conflict between Stalin and Trotsky

(Big Brother and Goldstein). The ideology of Airstrip One is Ingsoc—English socialism—and when the book became a success in the United States he had to issue a denial that this related to the postwar Labour government:

> My recent novel is NOT intended as an attack on Socialism or on the British Labour Party (of which I am a supporter) but as a show-up of the perversions to which a centralised economy is liable and which have already been partly realised in Communism and Fascism.[7]

Ingsoc, it might then be said, is no more English socialism than Minitrue is the Ministry of Truth. But the identification was in effect made, and it was profoundly damaging. Not in what it said about Soviet society—Orwell's position there was clear and consistent—but in what it implied generally about socialism and a "centralised economy." This connects with the most evident error in Orwell's projection: that the permanent and controlled war economy is shabby and undersupplied. The structural relations that we have since seen between a militarist economy and a controlled consumer affluence amount to more than a historical development that Orwell did not foresee. They indicate some of the social facts that, in what became an obsession with ideology, he did not take account of. There are good reasons why Orwell might not have foreseen an affluent and militarist capitalism, or a world of international corporations that functioned, internally and externally, very much like his projected Party. But he had the best of reasons—in direct experience—to know that political police, for example, were not

[7] *Collected Essays, . . . ,* IV, 502.

a socialist or communist invention; or propaganda, or censorship, or *agents provocateurs*. By assigning all modern forms of repression and authoritarian control to a single political tendency, he not only misrepresented it but cut short the kind of analysis that would recognize these inhuman and destructive forces wherever they appeared, under whatever names and masked by whatever ideology. For it would certainly, now, be *doublethink* to suppose that the only source of these elements is a form of socialism, just as only *thoughtcrime* could prevent us from seeing a propaganda phrase like "the free world" as a very clear example of Newspeak. In projecting an all too recognizable world Orwell confused us about its structures, its ideologies, and the possibilities of resisting it.

This point about resistance has a further importance when we remember Orwell's earlier work. At the most general level, his projection has undoubtedly been falsified. Under controls as pervasive and as cruel, many men and women have kept faith with each other, have kept their courage, and in several cases against heavy odds have risen to try to destroy the system or to change it. We can write Berlin, Budapest, Algiers, Aden, Watts, Prague in the margins of Orwell's passivity. He himself could have written St. Petersburg, Kronstadt, Barcelona, Warsaw. It would be right to acknowledge that many of the risings were defeats, but Orwell goes further, cutting out the spring of hope. He projects an enormous apathy on all the oppressed: a created mood, if ever there was one. Eighty-five per cent of the population are seen as an apathetic mass, and *proles*, as a description of them, seems more than Party jargon. The Party sees them as "natural inferiors . . . like animals," but how does Orwell see them? As a shouting, stupid crowd in the streets; drinking and gambling; "like the ant, which can see small objects but not large ones"; "people who had never learned to think." It is the world of working people as seen by the prep-school boy: "To me in my early boyhood, to nearly all children of families like mine, 'common' people seemed almost sub-human."[8] But, as in another early experience, this "almost sub-human" world can be seen, in a moment of revulsion from his own class, as the hope of the future, redeemers to be looked at with "mystical reverence": "people who had never learned to think but who were storing up in their hearts and bellies and muscles the power that would one day overturn the world."[9] "Out of those mighty loins a race of conscious beings must one day come."[10]

This stale revolutionary romanticism is as insulting as the original observation. It is the rising of the animals, as in the fable. "When you put it in words it sounded reasonable; it was when you looked at the human beings passing you on the pavement that it became an act of faith."[11] It needs to be said, however bitterly, that if the tyranny of 1984 ever finally comes, one of the major elements of the ideological preparation will have been just this way of seeing "the masses," "the human beings passing you on the pavement," the eighty-five per cent who are *proles.* And nobody who belongs to this majority or who knows them as people will give a damn whether the figure on the other side of the street sees them as animals to be subjected or as unthinking creatures out of whose

---

[8] *The Road to Wigan Pier*, p. 127.
[9] *Nineteen Eighty-four*, p. 226.
[10] *Ibid.*, p. 227.
[11] *Ibid.*, p. 89.

mighty loins the future will come. The incomplete humanity will be too clearly visible in the gesticulating observer himself.

That is how it goes, politically, throughout. Orwell had clearly seen the world of the power blocs, but the "hundreds of millions of ill-paid and hard-working coolies," inhabiting "the rough quadrilateral with its corners at Tangier, Brazzaville, Darwin and Hong Kong"[12] are also passive: "If they did not exist, the structure of world society, and the process by which it maintains itself, would not be essentially different."[13] It is a dreadful underestimate, not only of those people but of the structures of exploitation through which the metropolitan states are sustained. By viewing the struggle as one between only a few people over the heads of an apathetic mass, Orwell created the conditions for defeat and despair.

He continues his underestimate. He had seen people go back into Spain, under the threat of arrest, because of general and particular loyalties. He had seen hundreds of cases of fidelity under pressure. His wife had stayed in Barcelona, even lying in bed while the police searched her room, to be near him and to help him. But still

> Under the spreading chestnut tree
> I sold you and you sold me.

He can accurately describe this as "a peculiar, cracked, braying, jeering note . . . a yellow note"[14] but still it is what he makes happen. The cynical jingle of the rat race, which in similar forms we have been hearing ever since

12 *Ibid.*, p. 192.
13 *Ibid.*, p. 193.
14 *Ibid.*, p. 81.

from the agency offices and parties, leads straight to the nightmare of the rat in Room 101. Of course people break down under torture, but not all people break down. And in a filthy and repressive world there are deeper forms of personal resistance—as Orwell had reason to know—than the temporary affair between Winston and Julia.

The Party campaign against sex is one of the stranger elements of the projection (that it seems to have been taken from Zamyatin's *We* is relevant but secondary). The object of the campaign is to prevent uncontrollable loyalties but even more to "remove all pleasure from the sexual act." There have been such campaigns, though in some exploiting systems the first purpose can be achieved by a kind of abstract reversal of the second: pleasure without loyalty is even a marketable and institutional commodity. It is strange that Orwell could oppose the controls and the perversions with nothing better than the casual affair between Winston and Julia. This begins like the lovemaking trip to the country in *Keep the Aspidistra Flying*, but then it moves right away from any mutually recognizing personal experience:

> His heart leapt. Scores of times she had done it: he wished it had been hundreds, thousands. Anything that hinted at corruption always filled him with a wild hope.[15]

It is not the ordinary and continuing love of men and women, in friendship and in marriage, but a willed corruption or indifference—"the simple undifferentiated desire"—that is presented in opposition to (though it is usu-

[15] *Ibid.*, p. 129.

ally part of) that joyless world. Winston's marriage is a cold and miserable routine; only with the hint of corruption can the pleasure come.

Of the many failures in *Nineteen Eighty-four* this is perhaps the deepest. All the ordinary resources of personal life are written off as summarily as the *proles*. The lonely fantasy of "mighty loins" of the future is joined by the lonely confusion of the adolescent—so guilty about lovemaking that corruption of the object is a necessary element of its pleasure. Winston Smith is not like a man at all—in consciousness, in relationships, in the capacity for love and protection and endurance and loyalty. He is the last of the cut-down figures—less experienced, less intelligent, less loyal, less courageous than his creator—through whom rejection and defeat can be mediated.

The question about the view of the future in *Nineteen Eighty-four* is not an abstract one concerning the change from the optimism of Mercier or Wells to the pessimism of Huxley or Orwell. Abstract optimism and pessimism are almost equally beside the point, and there are plausible grounds for seeing a generalized future that is either dark or bright. What matters much more than the imposed general mood is the amount of experience drawn on. Promises or warnings that limit experience have limited relevance. So the question about *Nineteen Eighty-four*, as about Orwell's earlier novels, is why he created situations and people that, in comparison with his own written observations, are one-dimensional and determined. This is a matter not primarily of politics but of a more extended experience of self and society. Under the strength and sense of his only successful character, "Orwell"—a man physically and intellectually alive, conscious and tough and persistent—these feebler and less conscious figures moved in an undifferentiated theatrical landscape. The central significance is not in the personal contradictions but in the much deeper structures of a society and its literature. In making his projections, Orwell expressed much more than himself.

Continuities

vii

Soon after his death Orwell became, in effect, a symbolic figure. He was one of those men whose life and writing were in practice inseparable and who seemed to offer a style in which others could live and write. It would be easy to say that this was because he was a disillusioned, decent, and plain-living anticommunist: a figure the age needed. Of course the promotion of this image took place, but most people who had read him saw past it. He was not respected only by people who had given up their commitment to radical social change and who were using Orwell's disillusion as a cover. There were plenty of these, and others who didn't even have to live the process through, who could take Orwell's disillusion neat. But there were as many who began their political commitment at the point where Orwell left off, who agreed with him about Stalinism and about imperialism and the English Establishment, and who made a new socialist politics out of his sense of a failure.

There is a clear line, certainly, from "Inside the Whale" and *Nineteen Eighty-four* to an orthodox North Atlantic mood in which all humane and positive beliefs, especially a belief in radical change, were recognized in advance either as a projection of some personal or social maladjustment, or as an inexperienced, naïve, adolescent idealism, which despite the will and vision of its bearers led in practice straight to the authoritarianism that more sinister figures were all the time preparing. These explanations and warnings are still being confidently offered, sometimes with Orwell's name attached, as to the student movements of these past few years. Again, in some relation to this, there is certainly a clear line from Orwell's social thinking in "The Lion and the Unicorn" and similar essays to the British Labour Party revisionists of the 1950s and 1960s. The definition of socialism as the pursuit of equality had a traditional sound but a more precise contemporary significance: what had been understood as a socialist economy was (they argued) outdated by the development of an affluent industrial society; a new classlessness was emerging of its own accord and would be confirmed by measures of pragmatic social reform. Or, in Orwell's terms, "wrong members of the family," the old "feudal" or "aristocratic" elements, would be displaced by the new men, the "new Britain," and then the nation would become more civilized, more humane, more generally and equitably prosperous—just what Orwell had wanted as far back as *The Road to Wigan Pier*. This was akin to the feeling many radicals had who were not directly involved in the political arguments: a feeling that Orwell, unlike other socialist writers, understood English life—its pace, its tolerance, its distrust of abstractions and of theories pushed to extremes—a sensible, moderate, decent kind of life, which any hurried or drastic changes would disturb or put at risk, but which was still the basis for a steady extension of humane and responsible living.

We could call these views and moods Orwell's inheritance. But it is then all the more remarkable that the generation for whom Suez, Hungary, and the Bomb were signals for the renewal of political action looked to him with respect, a generation that believed not only in a new socialist movement but one based on disturbance: on demonstrations, on direct action, on the politics of the streets and the localities. This New Left respected Orwell directly, especially in its early years. The invasion of Suez was an open exercise of the British imperialism he had so consistently attacked. The Hungarian revolution, a popular and socialist rising against a bureaucratic and authoritarian communism, was at once a confirmation of what he had said about Stalinism and a demonstration of the authentic movement to which he had paid homage in Catalonia. The danger of the Bomb— "either we renounce it or it destroys us"—was as he had seen it: the Bomb was not only the weapon that could destroy civilization but the shadow under which a new authoritarian war economy would grow and extend. And then, closely involved with these political positions, there was the Orwell who had written about work, about poverty, about popular culture, the Orwell who had tried to live and feel where the majority of English people were living and feeling, reporting, understanding, respecting, beyond the range of an Establishment culture. These discernible elements of the New Left in Britain are, equally clearly, Orwell's effective legacy.

What kind of phenomenon is this, then, when the same man, the same writer, symbolizes such different tendencies, is appealed to and respected by opposing groups? It would be easy but pointless to start a quarrel over Orwell's legacy: it would be body-snatching or mantle-snatching; he would become a figure or a style to dignify his reputed successors. No useful analysis can go in for that. There has been too much of it already, in everything from anecdote to impersonation. "Father Knew George Orwell" is a cracked old song.

Nor is it very useful to attempt some reductive analysis. It would be easy to say that these different tendencies can be explained chronologically: the 1930s Orwell is the socialist, the 1940s Orwell the reactionary, the radical somewhere in between. But I have looked carefully through his writings, considering this explanation, and I am sure it doesn't work. Evidence for each of the positions can be drawn from each of the periods, though of course with differences of emphasis. There is the anti-imperialist of the early 1930s, the revolutionary socialist of the late 1930s, the radical essayist of the late 1930s and 1940s. Yet in the same periods there are the patterns of defeat; the figure of the isolated, honest man who has seen beyond the socialist talk; and the propagation of the myths of England. Or there is the disillusioned and embittered prophet of the 1940s, seeing progress as a swindle and revolution as self-defeating, but this man is also the radical essayist of the *Tribune* articles, active not only in defense of the victims of Stalinism but also in defense of "the civil liberties of any citizens of the British Empire," even including, despite his doubts and reservations, a man convicted for passing atomic secrets to the U.S.S.R.[1] That there are phases of Orwell's development is clear enough, but within each period there are some of the same contradictions.

A reductive analysis by forms of writing may again seem plausible but does not really work. Most radicals, I have noticed, prefer his essays, as if "The Art of Donald McGill" or "Dickens" or "How the Poor Die" or "Raffles and Miss Blandish" were somehow his major works. I admire these and many of the other essays, but I don't believe they can be isolated from his other work, and an Orwell restricted to them would be a much smaller figure. Or take the novels, up to *Coming Up for Air*. They have been much more influential than has been commonly noticed; indeed, one could say they created the style of the 1950s English novel of the drifting anti-hero, though themselves based on such diverse sources as Wells and Joyce, Gissing and Somerset Maugham. But the point is that all the contradictory tendencies are in the novels: the colloquial style and the seeking-out of ordinary life, but also the patterns of defeat, self-hatred, and that generalized swearing that covers reabsorption. In the journals and reporting there is usually a stronger and more consistent position, but some of the basic ambiguities are evident in almost everything but *Homage to Catalonia*. The creation of "Orwell"—the honest ob-

[1] *Collected Essays*, . . . , IV, 197, 377.

server—is more successful than the creation of the fictional characters, but we still have to explain the contradictions in that central consciousness.

Indeed the contradictions, the paradox of Orwell, must be seen as paramount. Instead of flattening out the contradictions by choosing this or that tendency as the "real" Orwell, or fragmenting them by separating this or that period or this or that genre, we ought to say that it is the paradoxes that are finally significant. No simple explanation of them will do justice to so complex a man (the more complex because he appears, on the surface, so plain). Some of the concepts we need for any full explanation may be beyond our reach just because of what we share with Orwell: a particular kind of historical pressure, a particular structure of responses and failures to respond. But two points can be suggested.

First, the key to Orwell as an individual is the problem of identity. Educated as he was to a particular consciousness, the key to his whole development is that he renounced it, or attempted to renounce it, and that he made a whole series of attempts to find a new social identity. Because of this process, we have a writer who was successively many things that would be unlikely in any normal trajectory: an Imperial Police officer, a resident of a casual ward, a revolutionary militiaman, a declassed intellectual, a middle-class English writer. And the strength of his work is that in the energy of his renunciation, he was exceptionally open to each new experience as it came. Different kinds of life flowed through him with only a minimal check from a more established identity, and the style he evolved—a studied simplicity, "letting the meaning choose the word"—shows that while

always traveling seriously, he is always traveling light. This quality can be related to his willingness to renounce his earlier attitudes and experiences and to write about them—or about others now with them—with contempt or anger, as if they were some other, quite separated thing. Yet in a period of exceptional mobility, this has positive as well as negative elements. Orwell could connect as closely and with as many different kinds of people as he did, precisely because of his continual mobility, his successive and serious assumption of roles. He dissolves himself into every situation and is thereby exceptionally convincing; his writing makes it easy for the reader to believe that this is also happening to himself. The absence of roots is also the absence of barriers.

It would be possible to say that this is the writer's "negative capability" of which Keats wrote. But there is no permanent psychology of "the writer." This is the social psychology of a particular kind of writer in a particular epoch. It is even, in Orwell's period, a class psychology. Aldous Huxley, W. H. Auden, Graham Greene, Christopher Isherwood, for all their differences, share with Orwell important elements of this position: traveling light and often, which is their overt social history; realizing others—other lives but especially other beliefs, other attitudes, other moods—through their own shifting negations. This structure of feeling is not what Keats meant by "negative capability"; it is at once sharper and smaller. The clarity and memorability of the successive realizations are an undoubted achievement, but there is also a characteristic coldness, an inability to realize the *full* life of another, a seeing of the other instead as a figure in all unrolling private landscape. In the case of Orwell, this coldness is most evident in his novels, where the presence of another as someone more than a stranger met or seen on a journey is expected and does not come. Relationships are characteristically meager, ephemeral, reluctant, dis-illusioning, even betraying, and this is very remarkable in the work of so generous a man. But one is sharply re-minded that in this at least Orwell was writing with the grain of his time. The relationships in his novels are char-acteristic relationships in the fiction of a period—a period marked by the certainty, even dogma, that this, now, is what all relationships are like. This is what I meant in saying that to describe the paradox of Orwell we would need concepts beyond the consciousness and the social structures of his period. All we can now propose is ex-perience: that there are other, fuller, more continuing relationships; that there are ways beyond even this aliena-tion.

Yet Orwell tried again and again to affirm, putting his life on the line. That is what makes him much more than a passive figure in this dominant structure of feeling. He shared it, but he tried to transcend it. As clearly as any-one in his generation, he sensed that this was, after all, a historical crisis, not a human condition or a metaphysical fact. His mobility, then, had a clear social intention. He was traveling light, but it was sureness of instinct, not chance, that took him to all the critical places and ex-periences of his epoch; and he was not only a visitor, either, but a man wanting and hoping to join in. He made a single life contain, at first hand, the experiences of im-perialism, of revolution, of poverty. He had no theory to explain them and no rooted positive beliefs extending beyond his own role. But with great stubbornness and persistence and courage he went to the centers of the history that was determining him, so that it might be experienced and differently determined. This, above everything, was his individual achievement. He was the writer who put himself out, who kept going and taking part, and who learned to write as a function of this very precise exploration.

But it is therefore more than an individual history. Nobody who shared or overlapped with his epoch can, in good faith, reduce his crisis to a personal development. There were important personal factors in his successes and failures, but some of the deepest contradictions are part of a shared history, and we cannot set ourselves above it, as if he were an abstract critical problem.

The second key to an understanding is, then, the nature of capitalist democracy in an epoch of socialist revolutions, of imperialism, of fascism, and of war. In the 1930s it was not difficult to see capitalist democracy in the context of political imperialism and economic depression. Its complicity with fascism, or, at best, its willingness to deal with fascism in a common opposition to socialism, could be seen not only in its dealings with the Soviet Union but in Spain. Reservation could be made about the nature of Soviet communism, or the internal politics of the Spanish Republic, yet a set of bearings held, or for many years seemed to hold. Capitalist democracy would not fight fascism, any more than it would liberate the colonial peoples or end the poverty that disfigured it in its own societies. Socialism had its profound internal differences and its own deep distortions, but it was the name, everywhere, for opposition to that dangerous and exploiting alliance.

Under massive historical pressures, in a very intricate process of cause and effect, this world-view was profoundly modified. The development of revolution in the Soviet Union and in Spain was itself deeply and bitterly affected by the character of the alliance against it and by its own desperate need for survival. Within a few years, what had seemed impossible became inescapable history: not only the further degeneration of Soviet communism, in the Stalin trials, and the betrayal of Spain, which were bitter enough, but the world-altering events of 1939: the pact between Stalin and Hitler and the beginning of war between fascism and the capitalist democracies. It may be easier, now, to gain some perspective on this process, to see the shadow of the incredible in the long earlier history of betrayal and default, the submerged contradictions coming at last into the open.

The most important effect, for anyone in Orwell's position, was the consequent response to capitalist democracy, for it was here that new contradictions and illusions were coming about almost unnoticed. For Orwell, the physical inevitability of the war against fascism combined first, as we have seen, with a traditional attachment to his country: Orwell's mature myth of England was written at just this point. But it was not just England that was in question, but the nature of capitalist democracy. In adjusting to England and to the war against fascism, it was easy to overadjust. "Capitalist," as a qualification of "democracy," could in effect be omitted or its reality underestimated, as it was in the illusion that the war against Germany could be turned into a revolutionary war, or as in the deeper, much more persistent illusion that it would be possible, quite quickly and without major disturbance, to bring the real England—democratic England—to the surface, breaking through the thin upper crust of an exhausted and archaic system. To the extent that "democracy" could be isolated, as in the alliance against fascism seemed plausible, it could be made the basis of an unanswerable criticism of a socialist order that under long historical pressures had become authoritarian. This would not have made so much sense if the experience of democracy had not been real, both in the inheritance of a liberal capitalism and in the bitterly fought-for freedoms of what was in effect a popular and anticapitalist culture. Physically it was there, its radically diverse elements confused and apparently inextricable. But in isolating the contrast between democratic and authoritarian regimes, abstracting them from the developing and contradictory character of their real social systems, a new set of illusions, a new and historically fragile world-view, was in fact prepared; it was, indeed, similar, in structure and effect, to the earlier isolation and abstraction of "socialism."

In other west-European countries, where elements of the old order collaborated with fascism and new alliances had to be made in the necessary resistance, other choices were possible. But in England capitalist democracy survived with its main contradictions intact, and then the pretense or hope that it was social democracy, or was about to become so, lasted longer than was good for anybody's reason. Even after the profound disillusions of 1945–1951 and 1964–1970, the pretense or hope survived. Yet no such illusion is static. If the only effective social contrast was between "democracy" and "communism," then some sort of accommodation with capitalism—that capitalism that was "on the point of" becoming a social democracy—was at first temporarily and then habitually conceivable. Having made this accommodation, and the corresponding identification of "communism" as the sole threat, it became harder to see and to admit what capitalist imperialism was still capable of doing: what, in the years since Orwell died, it has done again and again, in repression and in war.

This is the knot that was tied in the middle 1940s. And Orwell, indeed, helped to tie it. Then in his last fiction he discarded the apparently positive element of the illusion—the belief in the imminence of social democracy—and was left with only its negative effects. He could see only authoritarian communism, in the future, with no alternative or countervailing social forces. The first proposed title for what became *Nineteen Eighty-four* was *The Last Man in Europe*, and that is clearly how it felt. It has a certain bleak honesty, but it reveals a point at which the political contradictions, and the isolation and abstraction involved in them, combined with the lack of any independent social identity to produce a genuine terror.

This would not have got through to so many people if the contradictions had not been so general. But what in Orwell was a last desperate throw became for many others, absurdly, a way of life. His radical pessimism was combined with an accommodation to capitalism and with an illusion of the imminence of social democracy. What in Orwell broke down in terror became a comfortable and persistent world-view (in an older generation even lasting beyond Vietnam).

The only useful thing, now, is to understand how it

happened. In a confused and mobile history, his kind of loss of identity has continued to occur. The affiliation he tried to make, that he was ready to die for, was prevented by the political contradictions of those years and was lost, finally, in illusion and terror. The writer had to split from the political militant. Faith in the people had to be projected to an evolutionary distance, much farther than would ever have been necessary if his original class idea of unthinking subhumans had not translated so easily into a disillusioned view of the apathetic and tolerant mass. Beyond and past him, in and through many of the contradictions he experienced, real popular forces have continued to move, and the fight he joined and then despaired of has been renewed, has extended, and has gained important new ground.

We are never likely to reach a time when we can do without his frankness, his energy, his willingness to join in. These are the qualities we shall go on respecting in him, whatever other conclusions we may come to. But they are real qualities only if they are independent and active. The thing to do with his work, his history, is to read it, not imitate it. He is still there, tangibly, with the wound in his throat, the sad strong face, the plain words written in hardship and exposure. But then as we reach out to touch him we catch something of his hardness, a necessary hardness. We are acknowledging a presence and a distance: other names, other years; a history to respect, to remember, to move on from.

SHORT BIBLIOGRAPHY

Books by Orwell (in order of original publication)

Down and Out in Paris and London. New York: Harcourt, 1933.
Burmese Days. New York: Harper, 1934.
A Clergyman's Daughter. New York: Harcourt, 1960.
Keep the Aspidistra Flying. New York: Harcourt, 1956.
The Road to Wigan Pier. New York: Harcourt, 1958.
Homage to Catalonia. Philadelphia: Saunders, 1938.
Coming Up for Air. New York: Harcourt, 1950.
Animal Farm. New York: Harcourt, 1946.
Nineteen Eighty-four. New York: Harcourt, 1963.
Collected Essays, Journalism and Letters of George Orwell. Four volumes, edited by Sonia Orwell and Ian Angus. New York: Harcourt, 1968.

Some Books on Orwell

Atkins, John. *George Orwell.* New York: Ungar, 1965.
Brander, Laurence. *George Orwell.* Toronto: Longman, 1954.
Hollis, Christopher. *A Study of George Orwell.* Chicago: Regnery, 1958.
Hopkinson, Tom. *George Orwell.* London: Longman, 1953.

Rees, Richard. *George Orwell—Fugitive from the Camp of Victory.* Carbondale, Ill.: Southern Illinois, 1962.

Thomas, Edward M. *Orwell.* Edinburgh: Oliver & Boyd, 1953.

Vorhees, Richard J. *The Paradox of George Orwell.* West Lafayette, Ind.: Purdue University Studies, 1961.

Woodcock, George. *The Crystal Spirit.* Boston: Little, Brown, 1966.

I N D E X